LETTERS

ON THE

MINISTRY OF THE GOSPEL.

BY

FRANCIS WAYLAND.

BOSTON:
GOULD AND LINCOLN,
59 WASHINGTON STREET.
NEW YORK: SHELDON AND COMPANY.
CINCINNATI: GEORGE S. BLANCHARD.
1863.

ELECTROTYPED BY
W. F. DRAPER, ANDOVER, MASS.

To

DEACON HEMAN LINCOLN,

These Letters,

WRITTEN AT HIS URGENT SOLICITATION,

ARE RESPECTFULLY ADDRESSED,

BY

HIS FRIEND AND BROTHER,

THE AUTHOR.

CONTENTS.

LETTER I.

THE PAST AND THE PRESENT.

LETTER II.

A CALL TO THE MINISTRY.

LETTER III.

THE MINISTRY NOT A PROFESSION.

LETTER IV.

PREACHING THE GOSPEL. — THE CONVERSION OF SINNERS.

LETTER V.

PREACHING.—THE EDIFICATION OF BELIEVERS.

LETTER VI.

MANNER OF PREACHING.

LETTER VII.

PASTORAL VISITATION.

LETTER VIII.

OTHER PASTORAL DUTIES.

LETTER IX.

MINISTERIAL EXAMPLE.

LETTER X.

PERSONAL EXPLANATION. — CONCLUSION.

MINISTRY OF THE GOSPEL.

LETTER I.

MINISTRY OF THE PRESENT AND OF THE PAST COMPARED.

My Dear Brother:

YOU and I have frequently conversed on the subject of the Christian Ministry. We have compared the ministry of the present day with that of years long gone by. It has appeared to us both, that an important change has come over the character and labors of those who appear before men as the messengers of reconciliation. We seem to observe this in all denominations, but especially in that to which we belong. We have in the pulpit far more correct rhetoric than formerly; our ministers are better dressed, and much more familiar with the usages of society. The illustrations employed show that the preacher is familiar with modern literature, especially the literature of the English language. The terms of science and allusions to recent discovery are frequently used, either to enforce or explain the truths of the gospel. The worship of God by singing, accompanied by costly instruments, is frequently performed by salaried professional artists. Everything is in the highest degree decorous and proper. You may attend upon one of our churches for months without any danger of being offended by a single instance of false grammar. But little moral emotion is however aroused, nor does it seem to be much expected. On special occasions, on leaving the house of God you may hear the sermon applauded in terms such as these: "What a noble effort!" "That was a beautifully written discourse:" "What a brilliant train of thought!" "That sermon ought to be published; it would give reputation to our society." The sermon, however, excites no particular discussion. It gives rise to small self-inspection. No man asks himself, What have I done, or, What shall I do to be saved? It is a very rare occurrence for any hearer to be convicted by a sermon, or to be led by it to the cross of Christ. Such a result, as the immediate effect of preaching, seems neither to be labored for, nor anticipated. Of those who attend the worship of God, I fear that the greater part go because it has been their custom from youth. Some go for the respectability of the thing, others for the purpose of setting a good example, and all go expecting to hear a discourse on some serious subject to which a text from the Bible has been prefixed. This discourse is accurately written, and pleasantly delivered; tinged, it may be, with a reference to passing events, and sometimes with an allusion to authors that happen to be in vogue. If all this is successfully performed; if a fair proportion of the audience is wealthy and occupy a prominent position in society; if they pay their pew-tax freely and contribute respectably to the ordinary associations for benevolence; if they take good care of their minister, and provide liberally for his various seasons of recreation, the church is deemed to be in a flourishing condition. All this goes on year after year, and men seem hardly to suspect that these services were intended by Almighty God to be the means of rescuing them from hell and preparing them for heaven. The most that is accomplished is the pleasant occupation of the hour. Those who profess to be the disciples of Christ, and those who make no such profession, are equally at ease under the guidance of one who has assumed the care of their souls; while all are rapidly drawing near to the judgment-bar, and the great majority under the condemnation of the second death.

Sabbath schools commenced within the period

of our recollection, and they have since become universal. They have received the blessing of God, and from them come almost all the converts whose profession of faith gladdens the hearts of the pious. I sometimes fear, nevertheless, that even these are losing their efficiency as a means of moral training. I sometimes think that too much time is spent on incidentals, and not enough in the direct effort to bring souls to Christ. Geography, biography, and such subjects are liable to take the place of the doctrines of repentance and faith in Christ. Instead of acting mainly for the benefit of those who have no parents to instruct them, they in too many instances act mainly for the benefit of the members of the church and society; that is, for those whose parents would be greatly improved by teaching them themselves. The Sabbath school, however conducted, is coming to be considered the great means of the conversion of the world. The conversion of children is expected and prayed for. The conversion of adults is hardly anticipated, and very few means are taken to secure it. It would seem as if we were content, without an effort, to see them quietly pursuing the road which we know must lead to everlasting death.

Now we have known, in our early days, a very different condition of the ministry and the churches. We had then no magnificent, or even elegant, houses of worship. Our meeting-houses were frequently in out-of-the-way places, and difficult of access. They were at variance with taste, and by no means studious of comfort. We had no expensive instruments of music, and our singing was not at all of a high order; sometimes it was quite the reverse. The members of our churches were, for the most part, persons in the middle or lower walks of life. They had not the means of luxurious or expensive dress; and from this, or for better reasons, their dress was plain. I say for better reasons, for it was a common sentiment that it was unbecoming a disciple of Christ to acknowledge submission to the customs of the world, besides being injurious to a heavenly life. The social intercourse of the disciples of Christ was to a great degree confined to each other, and their conversation at these meetings was very commonly on the subject of religion. An evening spent in trivial conversation was considered as time wholly lost, and it left in the hearts of Christians a feeling of self-condemnation. In general, I think, it may be remarked that religion was a power which controlled the conduct of Christians in the various details of living, expenditure, and daily intercourse, much more than it is supposed to be at present.

Our ministry was of a much more diversified

character than it has been of later years. But few of our preachers had enjoyed the advantages of a classical education; and it was sometimes thought that these were not, in general, more efficient laborers than their brethren. In fact, there was, for a considerable period within my recollection, a prejudice against an educated ministry. It was supposed that an education far in advance of their brethren induced a reliance upon learning rather than on the Spirit of God. This was frequently carried to a ludicrous extreme. Some people believed that a man should not prepare for the pulpit by studying at all; and ministers would sometimes, in the way of boasting, declare at the commencement of a discourse that they did not know until they entered the pulpit from what text they should address the audience. The result was such as might be expected. They either spoke at random, without any object, and tending to no result, or else they had become familiar with one or two trains of thought, which they easily fell into, no matter what text they might happen to select. Not an uncommon feature in the preaching of the last generation, was a peculiar sing-song tone, which many ministers, and even educated men, were liable to contract. This has so entirely passed away from us that but few can understand what it is to which I refer. I believe that it still lingers in some portions of our country, especially among the Society of Friends. It was a very unpleasant, vehement sort of chanting, entirely artificial, and wholly at variance with any effort at good delivery. I am rather of the opinion that young extempore speakers were liable to fall into this habit from addressing large congregations, of which they stood in great fear. This sing-song took the place of that self-possession without which proper emphasis and the natural tones of emotion cannot exist; and when the habit was once formed, it generally continued through life. I have heard able and earnest sermons which have been rendered utterly distasteful by this vicious habit of delivery. Let us be thankful that this is a thing of the past.

Most of our ministers had received in youth the culture derived from common schools, and their acquisitions were more commonly made after their attention had been turned to the ministry. Occasionally they were wanting in taste, and in due appreciation of the relation existing between themselves and their audience. Their modes of expression and topics of illustration would sometimes grate sadly upon the ear; still there was decided power in their simple, honest earnestness. Others, of a more delicate mould, easily accommodated themselves to the circumstances in which they were placed. One of them, the late Rev. Alfred Bennet, has told me how he employed the time redeemed from labor, in studies at night by the light of pine knots; and how assiduously he attended courts in his neighborhood, for the purpose of observing the practice of lawyers, so that from them he might learn the best modes of public speaking, and the most successful manner of forming a popular argument. He became one of the best and most effective ministers and counsellors; and there is scarcely one of our number who was listened to with more general acceptance, or to whom the cause of mission's is under greater obligations.

It will be seen at once that such ministrations as these would not be attractive to the rich, to men of specially literary tastes, or men studious of social position. Men, women, and children inquiring what they should do to be saved; saints under doubts of the soundness of their hope of salvation, or striving to know how they might make progress in piety, however, flocked to hear them. In the country, as they preached when on a journey, or on a missionary tour, they were followed by such persons from school-house to school-house, and their labors were very commonly attended by a blessing. The plain, earnest ambassador of Christ spake out of the fulness of his heart, and as the Saviour promised: "He that believeth in me, out of him shall flow rivers of living water." Both ministers and people were content to be considered peculiar, and unlike the men who were living for this world. When sneered at and ridiculed, they believed it to be a fulfilment of the words of the Saviour: "Marvel not if the world hate you: if ye were of the world, the world would love its own; but because ye are not of the world, but I have chosen you out of the world, therefore the world hateth you." Yet the men who scoffed at what they esteemed their odious preciseness, confessed that they were honest and true-minded; that their word was as good as their bond; and if in alarming sickness they felt the need of prayer, or if in anguish on account of their sins they desired to know what they should do to be saved, these very outlandish disciples of Christ were the very persons whom they sought after. In fact, our brethren of the former generation were a people of a somewhat rugged character, having but little to do with the great world, and the more time to devote to religion: ready to bear their portion of the burdens of society, and forward, according to the standard of the time, in extending the knowledge of Christ; but neither seeking for the rewards of office, nor indeed were they often tempted by the offer of them. They stood aloof from political agitation. When a Christian man became a politician, it was a source of alarm to his brethren. I well remember to have heard it remarked, that since such or such a brother had become a politician, his Christian character and his interest in religion had sadly deteriorated; and his brethren feared that it would lead to his final apostasy.

If I have succeeded at all in conveying an idea of the character of our brethren in a former generation, it must be evident that in many important respects it differed from that of Christians of the present day. We have doubtless cast aside many of their errors, but may we not also have cast off many of their excellences? In swinging away from one extreme, have we not been in danger of vibrating towards the other? Might we not have avoided needless singularity, without in any respect lowering the standard of Christian character? While abstaining from giving cause of offence to the educated and cultivated, might we not still make it manifest, that though we are in the world we are not of the world, but in all conditions, and under all circumstances, we are never anything but witnesses for Christ? Let us consider this subject in the pure light of the word of God, and, I think, wisdom will be justified of her children.

It may be supposed that in speaking of the generation that has lately passed away, and also of that now living, I have fallen into exaggeration. If this be so, it is unintentional. The observation of one individual must be limited, and what may be true of one portion of our country may not be true of another. He can only tell of what has come under his own eyes, while the eyes of others may have taken a very different view. And besides, in looking over the events of their youth, and comparing them with the present, old men are particularly liable to error. The caution of the wise man on this subject is always to be held in memory by us who are advancing in years: "Say not thou what is the cause that the former days were better than these, for thou dost not inquire wisely concerning this." We are as liable to err in this respect as other men. We may, after all, be looking at this subject through the misty atmosphere which so commonly encompasses old age. Let us then throw aside our individual experiences, and ask, Is the case then closed? Is there no standard to which it is possible to appeal? If the present condition of the ministry and of the churches may not be compared with that of the period which preceded it, is there nothing by which its excellence or deficiency may be estimated? Let us consider this in another letter.

Yours, truly.

LETTER II.

A CALL TO THE MINISTRY.

MY DEAR BROTHER:

I THINK we may easily answer the questions at the close of my last letter in the affirmative. We need not ask whether the ministry of the present day is either better or worse than that of any other period. This inquiry does not reach the root of the matter. The only question of real importance is this: Is the ministry actually fulfilling the great purpose for which it was appointed? If it be anything more than a human device, it is an ordinance of God; and its character, and the objects of its institution, are to be learned from the pages of revelation. If the ministry is at present doing the work assigned to it in the New Testament, we need not ask whether or not it differs from that of a former generation. If it is not doing that work, and is becoming in any degree forgetful of the great object for which it was established, it is important that the facts should be known, and that we all should labor earnestly for its improvement.

Let us briefly recur to the facts which are commonly believed among us, and which are either plainly stated, or obviously taken for granted, on every page of the New Testament.

The New Testament, as we believe, distinctly teaches us that the whole race of man is in rebellion against the high and holy Ruler of the universe. Supreme love, that golden chain which unites all holy beings to God, is severed, and men "do not like to retain God in their knowledge." They are opposed to the pure and omniscient government of the Creator, and thus "the carnal heart is enmity against God." Truths respecting the claims of God and their obligations to him make no impression on the impenitent soul, any more than appeals to the senses affect a body from which the spirit has departed; or, in the language of the Scriptures, "they are dead in trespasses and sins." A being in such a moral condition can never be justified by his own merits; and therefore the law of God, holy, just, and good, can do nothing but utter his condemnation: for "by the law is the knowledge of sin," and "by the deeds of the law can no flesh be justified." A being thus at enmity with God must, unless something interpose, be banished from his presence, and such banishment is eternal death.

In this, our condition of helpless guilt, God, in unfathomable love, interposed and wrought out a way of salvation by which our sins might be pardoned, and our souls cleansed from moral pollution. "God so loved the world, that he gave his only begotten Son, that whosoever believeth on him should not perish, but have everlasting life." This salvation is prepared for the whole human race, and it is freely offered to all. Every one who has himself accepted it, is commanded to make known the good news to his brethren. "Go ye into all the world, and preach the gospel to every creature; he that believeth and is baptized shall be saved, and he that believeth not shall be damned." "The Spirit and the bride say, come; and let him that heareth say, come; and let him that is athirst come; and whosoever will, let him take the water of life freely." To every one who hears the gospel, the gate of heaven is as wide open as the gate of hell.

The duty of proclaiming this message of salvation is thus imposed upon every disciple of Christ. But lest, from the pressure of temporal business, it should be neglected, the Saviour has in every age chosen men out of the company of disciples, whose special calling it shall be, to labor for the conversion of souls. This was one part of the work for which the Son of God became incarnate; and he said to his ministers, "As my Father hath sent me, so send I you." The qualifications for the ministry are, by the Apostle Paul, spoken of as among the gifts which the Saviour, at his ascension, bestowed upon his disciples.

Thus the minister of Christ is a man appointed for a special service. The qualifications for his office are conferred on him by the ascended Saviour; and the matter of his teaching, and the object to be accomplished by it, are plainly set before him, in the word of God. Beyond these he cannot go; and if he does, he is preaching himself, and not Christ Jesus, his Lord.

I have said that God appoints men to this office, and hence it differs materially from any other trade or occupation. The latter, a man may assume for his own convenience, or profit, or taste, or love of ease. The former is by the appointment of God; and unless he be moved by the Spirit of God he may not undertake it.

But in what way does God appoint men to the ministry of the gospel? That he does appoint them in some manner, is, I think, evident from the passage just alluded to, where the apostle speaks of ministerial gifts as among the blessings bestowed on his church, in consequence of the ascension of Christ.

I answer: God, in the first place, qualifies men for this office by making them disciples of Christ, his renewed and obedient children, heirs of everlasting life. We can never suppose that God would employ men who are his enemies, in rebellion against him, to persuade others to be reconciled to him; that is, to do what they steadfastly refuse to do themselves. Unless a man have within himself the evidence that he has been born again, he has no right to enter the ministry. And on the other hand, unless a man give evidence by a Christian life that he is, in heart, a true disciple of Christ, no body of believers can, without sin, call him to the ministry.

The qualifications needful for the ministry are mentioned by the Apostle Paul, in his epistles to Timothy and to Titus. They are in these words: "A bishop (or, as it is in Titus, an elder) must be blameless; the husband of one wife; vigilant; sober; self-restrained; of good behavior; given to hospitality; apt to teach; not given to wine; no striker; not greedy of filthy lucre, but patient; not a brawler; not covetous; one that ruleth well his own house, having his children in subjection with all gravity; not a novice, lest, being lifted up with pride, he fall into the condemnation of the devil. Moreover, he must have a good report of them that are without, lest he fall into reproach and the snare of the devil." Many of these qualifications have reference to the temptations of heathenism, to which the first disciples were greatly exposed. We cannot, however, read this passage without observing that the apostle demands of a candidate for the ministry the evidence of established, consistent piety; a piety that shall manifest itself not only to his brethren, but to all that are without; and that in addition he be endowed with aptness to teach, or a capacity to instruct others, or the gift of public address. These qualifications were certainly quite unlike those commonly required by us in a candidate for the ministry. In explanation of this dissimilarity, it is common to refer to the difference of civilization which exists between the age of the apostles and our own. I cannot but suppose that this difference has been much exaggerated. The time of the apostles was toward the close of a period distinguished for writings which have for centuries been the classics of the civilized world. Rome, Corinth, Athens, Ephesus, Antioch, and Tarsus were, I apprehend, as cultivated, as acute, as tasteful, and as luxurious as London, Paris, New York, Boston, or Philadelphia; yet the directions for ordaining pastors were given with reference to several of those very places.

The Scriptures teach us, that when a man comes to us with a message from God, he must be moved to do so by God himself. The prophets who bore to the Jewish people warnings, or exhortations, or promises of forgiveness, always declared that they spake the words which were given them of God, and that they desired to speak nothing else. The apostles refer to their preaching in the same manner. St. Paul glories in the fact that, by exceeding grace, he was selected of God to be the dispenser of the riches of the gospel to the Gentiles. Nor was this confined to the apostles: the same Holy Spirit appointed to the work of the ministry the ordinary overseers or elders of the churches. Thus said Paul to the elders of the church of Ephesus, whom he met at Miletus: "Take heed, therefore, to yourselves, and to all the flock *over which the Holy Ghost hath made you overseers*, to feed the church of God, which he hath purchased with his own blood." The same doctrine was held by the reformers, as may be seen from the Book of Prayer of the Episcopal Church. In the ordination of deacons, the bishop demands of the candidate: "*Do you trust that you are inwardly moved by the Holy Ghost* to take upon you this office and ministration, to serve God for the promotion of his glory, and the edifying of his people?" The candidate must answer: "I trust so." I suppose this to be the uniform belief of all the denominations who hold the doctrines taught at the Reformation.

But in what manner does the Holy Spirit make it known to a man that it is his duty to devote himself to this special service? He cannot expect that God should speak to him in an audible voice. The Holy Spirit does not address men in that way. He must then, as the Prayer-Book has it, be "*inwardly* moved." By this I mean that the Holy Spirit so sets before a man his duty to serve God in this manner, that he can with a good conscience serve him in no other. It is not enough that, having surveyed the several modes of life open before him, he prefers this one because his intellectual tastes lead him in this direction, or that he may thus enjoy a life of ease and literary leisure, or because if he chooses this calling he can enter it with greater ease than any other. These are selfish and worldly considerations, such as the Holy Spirit never puts into the minds of men. On the contrary, he to whom the Holy Spirit makes known that this is his duty, is, in the first place, rendered willing to serve in any manner that God shall see fit to designate. He lays himself and all that is most dear to him on the altar, and, with Saul at Damascus, only asks: "Lord, what wilt thou have me to do?" This is the proper state of mind for every disciple of Christ. When this question is asked in humility and simple sincerity, I believe that there are some men who see the ministry of the gospel set before them as the only service in which they can please God. It is not for any temporal advantage that they choose it. It may lead to sacrifices, self-denials, the surrender of many a cherished project, the suffering of much that flesh and blood would gladly escape; but all this matters not. The voice of God has said to the man: "This is the way, walk thou in it"; and come what will, he dares not walk in any other. The way may seem dark to him, but from time to time the promise whispers, "Lo, I am with you always"; and with his whole heart he surrenders himself cheerfully to the service of Christ, in the ministry of the word.

But it will be said a man may easily mistake the intimations of the Spirit. He may entertain erroneous conceptions of his qualifications for the ministry, and thus place himself in a position from which he can neither advance nor retreat without apparent disgrace. This is doubtless true. Many have made this mistake, and never has it been more frequently made, than when the view of a call to the ministry such as I am advocating is very much forgotten. How many quite young men, ignorant of their own qualifications, attracted, perhaps, by the apparent pleasantness of the calling, or moved by the injudicious advice of friends, are annually placed in a course which must end either in the ministry or disgrace! How many of those who have consumed eight or nine years in preparation for the ministry, find, when it is too late, that they have mistaken their calling, and that the best part of their lives has been spent to no purpose! They find that preaching is not their vocation, and to enter upon a wholly secular calling is almost impossible. A sort of medium course is taken, by which they may labor in some good cause without ostensibly relinquishing the ministry. Hence all sorts of places are filled with ministers, without charge, who have devoted their lives to some other object than the preaching of the gospel. Colleges, academies, schools, derive their instructors, in a large proportion, from men who have been educated for the ministry. Agents for colleges, solicitors for their funds, and for the funds of all our benevolent associations, are taken from our educated clergy. Editors of religious newspapers, and a large part of the staff of such an establishment, are taken from the same class. In most of our benevolent associations the paid offices are held by clergymen, except that of treasurer, which is always held by a layman. The circulation of religious books, in various forms, is done by the same class of men. In view of these facts, it is evident that many who prepare for the ministry have mistaken their calling, and therefore a liability to this mistake is not peculiar to the view which I have taken.

But this is not all. It is not enough that the man believes himself called to this work; it yet remains that his brethren see in him the proper qualifications. The necessity of such consent of his Christian brethren is acknowledged in all denominations. Sometimes the judgment in this case is left to the church of which the candidate is a member, to be, in case of ordination, confirmed by a council; or it is left with a presbytery, a body composed of ministers and laymen from the vicinity; or it rests with the presiding elders and bishops in the Methodist, or with the bishop and standing-committee in the Episcopal Church. In the latter church, the candidates are presented to the bishop by a minister or ministers, who are addressed by him as follows: "Take heed that the person (or persons) whom ye present unto us be apt and meet for their learning and godly conversation, to exercise their ministry duly to the honor of God and the edifying of his church." The minister answers: "I have inquired concerning them, and also examined them, and think them so to be." These two evidences then, — the conviction in the mind of the candidate that he is "inwardly" called to the work, and the belief of his brethren that he possesses the proper qualifications, — seem to be generally required by all Protestant Christians. Such, at least, is our theory; whether or not our practice conforms to it, those who are best acquainted with the facts can answer.

There is, however, in both cases, presupposed, a

conviction of the most solemn responsibility. Both are supposed to speak and act in view of their accountability to God. If the candidate utters these words as a mere form, if he declares himself "inwardly moved by the Holy Ghost" to undertake this work, while he is destitute of any such consciousness, or, if those who give him their sanction do it without inquiry, examination, or satisfactory knowledge of his qualifications, then the party or parties so acting are guilty of lying to the Holy Ghost. If both parties act as it becomes men under such responsibility, there will be no great danger of mistake. A fallible being will fail somewhere; but there is here as little liability to failure as falls to men in any of the ordinary affairs of life.

Yours, truly.

LETTER III.

IN WHAT SENSE IS THE MINISTRY OF THE GOSPEL A PROFESSION?

MY DEAR BROTHER:

I THINK you must have observed a change which has taken place, within the period of your recollection, in the terms which are used in speaking of the ministry. It has become common to class the ministry with what are called the liberal or learned professions, especially those of law and medicine. Thus a young man will frequently speak of the profession which he shall choose, compare the various agreeables and disagreeables of each, deliberately weighing the rate of compensation of each, and measuring the opportunity which each offers for mental improvement, and for ease and comfort in living.

After it has been taken for granted that the ministry of the gospel is a liberal profession, standing on the same ground as other professions, the question naturally arises, why should not the same rules of conduct apply equally to all? Thus the lawyer, or physician, who has spent time and money in his professional education, feels perfectly at liberty to labor where he shall receive the largest compensation: why should not a minister do the same? Professional men, if they can command the means, consider it appropriate to live in ease and luxury: why should this profession be an exception? Men in other professions, if their engagements will allow it, cast off the cares of business, and spend some part of the year in physical enjoyment at places of fashionable resort: why should not a minister do likewise? The leading members of a church or congregation in a city frequently spend a year or two in visiting the cities of Europe, looking at paintings and sculpture, gazing at buildings, and attending various public exhibitions of artistic excellence: why should not a pastor indulge himself in these enjoyments as well as his people; and if the means are provided for him, why should he not avail himself of the opportunity? The families of professional men enter commonly into what are called the innocent gayeties of life, and thus unite with the opulent in forming a caste for themselves: why should not the family of a minister enjoy this privilege when it is proffered to him? All these questions naturally arise after it is taken for granted that the ministry is a profession,—that is, a way of earning a living by the labor of the mind rather than of the body, — and entitled to all that is common to those who obtain their living in this manner. I say these questions will naturally arise. I say more: if we grant the premises, we must answer them all in the same manner.

But let us go back a little. Is the gospel a profession, in the sense in which this word is commonly understood?

There is one point of view, and only one, from which there is seen any analogy between the ministry of the gospel, and the professions of which we have spoken. The term profession is commonly used to designate those callings whose object it is to teach us the laws by which we should regulate our conduct in the various circumstances of life. The lawyer teaches us how to avail ourselves of the laws of the land, for the purpose of obtaining our rights and redressing our wrongs. The physician teaches us how to obey the physical laws under which we are created, so that we may preserve our health, or regain it when it has become impaired. The minister of religion teaches us how we may secure the favor of God and prepare in this life for the life that is to come. In this respect there is a general analogy between all these callings, and therefore the political economist places them in the same class of laborers.

In every other respect, I think, the ministry differs essentially both from the professions and every other calling in life.

1. In the selection of any other occupation than that of the ministry, a man is governed by his own individual choice. He follows the bias of his own mind, or the dictates of expediency; he chooses that which opens the most promising field for the display of his own peculiar talent, or which will, in the shortest time, secure for him competence or opulence, or which will lead most directly to political eminence, if perchance he has bowed down to that seductive idol. Having settled those questions satisfactorily to himself, he forms his decision, and acts accordingly; he has nothing further to ask, and he is satisfied that his inquiries have covered the whole ground.

With the minister of the gospel of Jesus Christ it is entirely different. He does not enter upon this calling because it will lead to temporal advancement, to ease, or wealth, or power, or because it will gratify his desire for intellectual investigation, or afford occasions for the cultivation of taste; he undertakes this service because he believes that he is "inwardly moved to do so by the Holy Spirit." The conviction is fastened upon his conscience that he must do it or he will displease God, and that in no other course of life can he ask for his blessing. He feels that God has spoken to him, and he dares not disobey. Other callings are chosen from views of mere temporal expediency; this is undertaken in obedience to the commands of God, addressed to his individual soul.

2. The relation of the professional man to his employers, is essentially that of principal and agent. The employer is the principal; the lawyer or physician is the agent. His services are required for the purpose of doing for the principal what he cannot do for himself. If the agent faithfully serves his principal, and the principal honorably pays the agent, the whole case is closed. So far as the professional relation is concerned, it is a contract exclusively between the two parties; and, when each has performed faithfully his part of the agreement, we look for nothing beyond.

But the ministry of the gospel is of a totally different character. The minister is an agent, but his principal is neither client nor patient, nor congregation, but Almighty God. He is appointed of God to perform a special service, and to God is he responsible. He may preach so as to please his congregation; they may pay him punctually and liberally; they may applaud his efforts, and be proud of his talents, while both he and they, in this very thing, are odious in the sight of God; and he, especially, who has undertaken the cure of their souls, may be fixing upon himself the doom of the unprofitable servant. God has sent him to deliver his message to this people; has he delivered it? He may have all the while been delivering something else, or he may have delivered something like it, but so modified to please his hearers, or gain for himself a reputation, that God never acknowledges it as his communication to sinful men. The command of the Master is, that he preach the preaching which the Spirit gives him, whether men will hear, or whether they will forbear; and if he do not obey the command, however much men may applaud, he can expect nothing but the frown of an offended God.

And hence, though he make a contract with his people as to the kind and amount of his labor, this is no justification in the sight of God. This cannot annul the command which God imposed upon him when he undertook this service. His people may be willing that he should preach only so often in the week; that he should never visit them for the purpose of religious conversation; and that for so long a time in the year he should be free from all pastoral labor. His brethren, at his ordination, besides urging upon the people the very proper duty of paying him punctually, may teach them that they must not expect him to spend his time in pastoral visitation, but take it for granted, that, if he do not perform this labor, he is deeply engaged in study for their benefit, pouring out his soul with strong crying and tears for their conversion. All this may be done, but yet it alters not the case. His principal is neither his people nor his brethren, but the ascended Saviour; and at the last day he will find it to be a small thing to be judged by man's judgment. He that judgeth him is the Lord.

When Paul was bidding farewell to the church at Ephesus, with whom he had labored as pastor for three years, he did not place his confidence that he was free from the blood of all men on the ground that he had kept the pulpit regularly supplied, and had done everything that they had employed him to do; nor did they take comfort to themselves that they had paid his salary quarterly, and in acts of kindness had gone even beyond their engagement. The apostle's retrospect of his services, and of the account which he was to render, was of another kind. "Ye know," said he, "from the first day that I came into Asia, after what manner I have been with you at all seasons, serving the Lord with all humility of mind, and how I kept back nothing that was profitable unto you, but have showed you and taught you publicly, and from house to house, testifying both to the Jews and to the Greeks repentance towards God, and faith towards the Lord Jesus Christ. Neither count I my life dear to myself, so that I might finish my course with joy, and the ministry which I have received of the Lord Jesus, to testify the gospel of the grace of God. Wherefore I take you to record this day, that I am pure from the blood of all men; for I have not shunned to declare to you the whole counsel of God. Take heed to yourselves, and to the whole flock over which the Holy Ghost hath made you overseers, to feed the flock of God which he hath purchased with his own blood. Therefore watch; and remember that by the space of three years I have not ceased to warn every one, day and night, with tears. I have coveted no man's silver, or gold, or apparel; ye yourselves know that these hands have ministered unto my necessities, and those that were with me. I have showed you all things, how that so laboring ye ought to support the weak; and to remember the words of the Lord Jesus, It is more blessed to give than to receive."

Again, the rewards promised in the New Testament to the minister of the gospel, are not temporal, but eternal. They were warned by the Saviour to expect from the world persecution, and every form of ill-treatment. This was declared to be the lot of all the disciples. So, at the close of his life, Paul declared that all who will live godly in Christ Jesus must suffer persecution. The normal relation of the church to the world renders this almost a necessity. Jesus intends his disciples to be, in the practice of every virtue, far in advance of the world that lieth in wickedness. But to be thus in advance of the world, and by precept and example to bear testimony against its prevailing practices, must, of course, arouse its ill-will. This may show itself in various ways, according to the progress of civilization and the more perfect knowledge of the rights of man. In the times of the Apostle, the Jews stoned and the Romans beheaded or crucified a faithful preacher of Christ. In the times of Whitfield, they assaulted him with dead cats and rotten eggs. At other times, uncompromising and consistent obedience to Christ will occasion many a cold look, frequent accusations of fanaticism and hypocrisy, and an eagerness to fabricate and hear and believe anything to his disadvantage. At times when the profession of religion has degenerated into formalism, it not unfrequently happens, that to the contradiction of sinners there is added the contradiction of saints. For a large share of this ill-will, the minister who fearlessly inculcates the obligation to live a godly and self-denying life, and urges upon all men the necessity of repentance and faith in Christ as absolutely necessary to salvation, must prepare himself. Observe the evidences of a true ministerial character in the view of the Apostle of the Gentiles: "In all things approving ourselves as the ministers of God, in much patience, in afflictions, in necessities, in distresses, in strifes, in imprisonments, in tumults, in labors, in watchings, in fastings: by pureness, by knowledge, by long-suffering, by kindness, by the Holy Ghost, by love unfeigned, by the word of truth, by the power of God, by the armor of righteousness on the right hand and on the left, by honor and dishonor, by evil report and good report: as deceivers, and yet true; as unknown, and yet well known; as dying, and behold we live; as chastened, and not killed; as sorrowful, yet always rejoicing; as poor, yet making many rich; as having nothing, yet possessing all things."

It has sometimes occurred to me that the evidences by which a clergyman might at the present time show that he had been a successful minister of Christ, would be somewhat unlike those of the Apostle Paul. It might be something like this: "At an early age I lost both of my parents by death, and, after obtaining the advantages of a common-school education, was under the necessity of earning my own living. While thus occupied, during a revival in my native town I became, as I trust, the subject of divine grace, and entered upon a Christian life with all the zeal of a new convert. I frequently spoke and prayed in the meetings of persons of my own age. Soon, to my surprise, the older brethren in the church urged me to prepare for the ministry. Being destitute of the means for procuring an education, they assured me that by the aid of the Education Society, together with that of Christian friends, I might, without difficulty, be carried through a course of classical and theological education, and, under the best auspices, enter the ministry of the gospel. I had never thought of the subject until it was suggested to me, but the proposal was too flattering to be disregarded. I was at once liberated from my previous engagement, and entered the academy at A.

"Here I found myself in the midst of young men quite unlike those with whom I had previously associated, and I painfully felt my deficiencies. Being fond of study, however, and possessing, perhaps I may say without vanity, somewhat more than the usual facility for acquisition and adaptation, I was soon able to place myself on a par with the best of them. In due time I left the academy, with flattering testimonials, and entered the college at B.

"At college I maintained the standing I had already acquired, and, to quote the words of the apostle, profited above many that were my equals. I regret, however, to say, that my religious principles did not here gain either in depth or earnestness. I felt that I was for the time preparing for future usefulness by intellectual improvement, and that this must be the object of my greatest solicitude. My officers of instruction were all professors of religion, and some of them clergymen; but they seemed to think their duty discharged when they had awakened in us a love of science and letters, and during my whole residence but one of them ever conversed with me on the subject of personal religion. My piety suffered in consequence, though I was guilty of no immoral conduct, and was a frequent attendant upon the meetings for prayer. I must, however, confess, that bearing the cross for Christ had not many practical advocates among us. At the close of my course I received an appointment which gratified my friends, and graduated with the reputation of being a correct disciple of Christ.

"At the seminary, which I immediately entered, my religious life was, in most respects, the same. At first, the thought that I was now irrevocably committed to the ministry, produced in me a feeling of solemnity. I prayed more frequently and more earnestly, and strove to consecrate myself anew to God. Soon, however, I became more than ever absorbed in study, and these feelings gradually subsided. The kind of places most to be desired in the ministry, was a frequent subject of our conversation, and I labored assiduously to prepare myself for a prominent position in our church. Nor was my labor wholly in vain. I received several invitations to preach, as a candidate, as soon as my theological course was completed. I settled at once in the flourishing village of C., at a salary of one thousand dollars per annum. I preferred this to a more public situation because its duties were not oppressive, and I should have leisure to pursue with less interruption the studies which I had commenced, and thus prepare for more extended usefulness. Here I succeeded in building up a prosperous society, and, beyond my merits, was esteemed one of the most promising ministers in that vicinity.

"I had been seven years pastor of the church at C., when I received a call from a church in the city of D., one of the most wealthy societies of our denomination in that metropolis. The salary was such, and the field of usefulness so great, that the call seemed irresistible. It placed me at once in affluence, while the labor, beyond preparation for the Sabbath, was left very much at my discretion. The miscellaneous business of such a position I knew to be great, but I was at liberty to undertake as much or as little of it as I chose; and I suppose I have rather an aptitude for executive affairs. I was always earnest in the cause of education, and succeeded in inducing my church, a few years after my settlement, to establish a professorship in the college at which I was graduated. At the following commencement, to my astonishment, I was honored with the degree of Doctor in Divinity. My people have twice sent me to Europe, paying all my expenses. They allow me as much time as I desire for recreation, by which means I have been in the enjoyment of excellent health. My house is in one of the pleasantest parts of the city, and is as well furnished as that of professional men generally. In my family I have been greatly blessed. Two of my sons occupy prominent positions: one as a lawyer, and the other as a partner in a most respectable mercantile house. The youngest has entered the ministry, and has for some time been settled in the city of E. My two daughters are both well married, and I am surrounded with every blessing which the kindness and respect of the community can confer. Through the blessing of God, I am permitted to look back on my life and thank him for leading me into the ministry; for rendering that ministry so successful, and bestowing on me so many tokens of his favor. I could not have been happier had I chosen any other profession. Bless the Lord, O my soul! and forget not all his benefits."

I ask, would not this be considered a very successful ministry? Is it not, however, greatly unlike that of St. Paul? The one represents the apostolic, the other the professional view of the minister of the gospel.

But we may consider this subject from a somewhat different point of view. We may profitably reflect on the terms by which the ministry is designated, and the human callings with which it is most in analogy. We observe, then, that the minister of Christ is, in the New Testament, frequently called a steward; that is, the upper servant in a large household, whose principal duty it is to distribute to the other servants their daily provisions. Thus the apostle addresses the Corinthians: "Let a man so account of us as ministers of Christ, and stewards of the mysteries of God. Moreover, it is required of stewards that a man be found faithful." "But with me it is a very small thing that I should be judged of you, or of man's judgment: yea, I judge not mine own self; for I know nothing of myself [that is, I have no consciousness of acting unfaithfully], yet am I not hereby justified. He that judgeth me is the Lord." The apostle frequently in his epistles refers to this view of his office. He exults that the dispensation of the gospel — that is, the duty of dispensing it as a steward — is committed to him.

A steward is the person in the household to whom the master commits the duty of distributing to the servants the provisions needful for every day. That which he distributes is wholly the property of his proprietor, not a particle of it belongs to himself; and if he use any of it for his personal advantage, he is an unfaithful servant. In distributing it among his fellow-servants, he has no right to make use of anything that has not been put into his hands for this purpose. He has power over that committed to him, and no more; but what has been thus committed he must distribute to the last atom, for it is required of stewards that a man be found faithful. His fellow-servants may desire something more, or something different, but he dares not listen to them for a moment. They may dislike the food, and ill-treat him because he will not yield to their wishes. But all this matters not; his account is not to be rendered to them, but to his master; and therefore it is a small thing to be judged by their judgment. Nay, though he is conscious of no intentional error, yet, having to render his account to one who will examine it with the most scrupulous exactness, he frequently trembles lest at last he should be found wanting.

Thus is it with the minister of Christ. He is entrusted by the Master with the duty of dispensing to his fellow-men the truth which God has revealed to them; but especially with the news to a perishing world of salvation by the blood of

Christ. They are not his own ideas, but the ideas of God. He must deliver them all, keeping back nothing. He must communicate them to others just as he receives them from the holy oracle. His fellow-men may like a part and not the whole, or they may prefer something different; but it all matters not: he must dispense precisely what has been committed to him in the written word, through the illumination of the Holy Spirit. His account has not to be rendered to them, but to God, who trieth the heart; therefore it is a small thing to be judged by them, or of man's judgment. God has entrusted him with the good news of salvation, and this he must make known in simplicity and godly sincerity to all men; for every child of Adam must perish without it. He must do this everywhere, with unshrinking faithfulness. What men may think of him is a very trifling matter. It can neither condemn nor justify him, for it is not before their tribunal that he is to appear. Nay, though aware of no dereliction in duty, he dares not rely on his own consciousness of rectitude as a justification before an all-seeing God. Having done all, he casts himself and all his services at the foot of the cross, that, sprinkled with atoning blood, they may, through the merits of the Saviour, be accepted, having been cleansed through him from all imperfection.

But we must go further, and reflect on the relation which the gospel steward sustains to his fellow-men. He is sent to men perishing by famine and dying around him. The food which he dispenses is all that has ever been given for the supply of their wants; aside from it there is no possible provision. They, however, have no appetite for the food which he has to dispense, nor any confidence in the benevolent proprietor who has sent him. The duty of the steward, then, is not completed when he has merely set the food before them. He must, by every means in his power, strive to persuade them to partake of it, and "compel them to come in." No matter who they are,—rich or poor, young or old, wise or unwise, learned or ignorant, —all are perishing, and he must endeavor to save them all. He must use every means to show to them their danger; he must convince them that their necessity admits of no delay; he must teach them the character of the benevolent proprietor; he must exhibit to them the effect which the food which he offers has produced upon others; and above all exemplify the effect which it has produced upon himself, once perishing like themselves, but now enjoying all the vigor of spiritual health, and never cease until he sees them turn their fainting eyes toward the rich provision that has been made for them, eat it, and live forever. Would the

authority of God, and is, at this moment, in rebellion against him. He has provided a most merciful way for their return to their allegiance, and has sent his ministers as ambassadors to offer them terms of reconciliation. The instructions by which they are to be governed in this embassy are made known in the New Testament. These they have no authority to enlarge, abridge, alter, or modify. They are to make them known to all men, in all plainness and simplicity. All are engaged in this rebellion, and to all, young or old, polished or rude, learned or unlearned, the message of God is to be delivered. If the professed minister of Christ propose any terms not offered by his Sovereign, or if he fail to make them known in all clearness, or if he clothe them in language which cannot be understood, the souls of men are lost, and he must be responsible to his Sovereign. If, especially, he make the delivery of this message the means of securing personal advantage, instead of faithfully making known the will of the Master, he is false to his trust; and the souls of sinners, which he has bartered away for the applause of men, will be required at his hands.

But the case of the ambassador of Christ has some peculiarities. The ambassador ordinarily is commissioned to a government, and all his dealing is with it, and not at all with individuals.

He must make his communication to the officers of state, and to them exclusively. Not so with the ambassador of Christ. In the Old Testament we find nations addressed, and the communications from God are to them, and especially to their rulers. In the New Testament we perceive nothing of the kind; and but for the fact of persecutions, we should have no mention of nations as such, or of the magistrates who governed them. The gospel of Jesus Christ is a communication made from God to *each individual* of the human race. It is good news to be made known to *every creature.* The ambassador is therefore sent with his message, not to collective masses, but to every individual soul.

And again, an ambassador among men is commissioned *to make known* to those to whom he is sent, simply the message of his sovereign. He has no command to *persuade* them to accept of the terms which he offers. When he has, in faithfulness and kindness, made them known, his duty is accomplished, and the responsibility rests with them. But with the ambassador of Christ the case is different. The Sovereign who has sent him, the eternal God, has manifested the most intense desire that our rebellious race should be reconciled to him. He has made the most costly offering in the universe to render our return to him possible. He has sent his Holy Spirit to impress the truth upon the consciences of men, and having done all this, — oh, infinite condescension! — he draws near, and beseeches us to be reconciled to him. The ambassador of such a Father in heaven to his erring and lost children has far more to do than *officially to deliver* his message. He is the messenger to man of a beseeching God. Can he do less than devote his whole energy to the work of persuading men to return to their Father in heaven? The gospel feast is prepared, and he is sent to scour the country — to go to the "highways and hedges, and compel them to come in." At home and abroad, publicly and from house to house, among the poor and despised as much as among the rich and the powerful, among the young and the old, he is everywhere to plead with men to be reconciled to God. By every motive derived from the law by which we are to be judged, from the holiness and the love of God, from the self-sacrificing compassion of our Lord Jesus Christ, from the fulness and freeness of the offer of salvation, from the eternal realities of a world of happiness and a world of woe, he is to urge men to be reconciled to God through the death of his well-beloved Son. In a word, the ambassador of Christ is to devote his whole being to the work of preparing souls for heaven, to the conversion of men from sin to holiness, presenting them "without spot or wrinkle, or any such thing, before the throne of God."

Is this any more than a simple, though very imperfect statement of the duties of the ministry of the gospel, as they are made known in the word of God? Is it, in any respect, exaggerated? If in any, in what? It is not exaggerated; for no language can exaggerate its responsibility. We all know the solemn errand on which the Son of God visited our earth; and he himself has said, "As my Father has sent me, so send I you." We are sent to do the same work (the atonement of course excepted) for which God became incarnate, and who is sufficient for these things?

Is this work, then, to be accomplished by weekly lectures on some social duty, enforced from the teaching of natural conscience; or by a view of the benefits which will accrue to the community by the performance of it; or by a lifeless demonstration of some doctrine of revelation, in the practical application of which neither speaker nor hearer seem to have any more interest than if both were inhabitants of the planet Jupiter; or by reading a discourse on something collateral to religion, in which the name of Jesus is never spoken, if even referred to; or by a description of some locality in Judea, with allusions to the several classes of individuals to whom the gospel was first delivered; or by an eloquent amplification of truisms which no one ever disputed; or by entertaining an audience for an hour or two every Sabbath, without bringing home to their consciences their obligations to repent and believe; or, in a word, by so preaching that a careless sinner might attend our ministrations for months together without once being brought face to face with his own conscience, or a convicted sinner be pointed to the Lamb of God that taketh away the sins of the world? Let any man read the New Testament, and then judge for himself whether this is doing the work of an ambassador of Christ to a revolted and perishing world. Was this the way in which the Apostle Paul did the work of a pastor at Ephesus or Corinth, cities as renowned as any at the present day for learning, intelligence, or refinement? Let him answer for himself: "And I, brethren, when I came unto you, came not with excellency of speech or of wisdom, delivering unto you the testimony of God, for I determined to preach nothing among you but Jesus Christ and him crucified; and I was with you in weakness and fear, and in much trembling, and my speech and my preaching was not with enticing words of man's wisdom, but in demonstration of the Spirit and of power." In this way did the apostle build up a church in the city of Corinth.

Looking at the ministry of the gospel from this point of view, how is the office degraded when we speak of it as a profession, or when we derive our rules for the discharge of its duties from any calling upon earth! Suppose an ambassador from any court of Europe should appear among us, and, declaring himself a professional man, should measure his duties and responsibilities by the rules which governed the lawyers and physicians at Washington? Could words express the contempt which he would inspire in the breasts of the people to whom he was sent, or in the mind of him who commissioned him? Peace or war, the happiness or misery of millions, depend on the manner in which he discharges his duty; and, forgetful of all this, he yields himself up to the manners of the men by whom he is surrounded. He will neither read nor write a despatch, he will neither make nor attend to a communication, if it will interfere with his attendance at a ball or the betting at a horse-race. We, as ministers of the gospel, claim to be the ambassadors of the Sovereign of the universe to our lost fellow-men. If we make such a claim, let us act in a manner that shall correspond with it.

Yours, truly.

LETTER IV.

PREACHING THE GOSPEL.—THE CONVERSION OF SINNERS.

My Dear Brother:

WE have delayed long enough on the professional aspect of the ministry: let us proceed to consider this calling from another point of view.

The duties of a minister beseeching men to be reconciled to God are of three kinds: First, public, or preaching; second, private conversation with individuals; and thirdly, exemplary, or the manifestation of the truth by his daily life. These are all demanded by the nature of his office. He cannot fully discharge his duty unless his influence is felt in all these directions.

Let us, then, first consider that part of a minister's duty which is discharged in the pulpit, or preaching.

The object of the ministry, then, is, in the first place, to persuade men to be reconciled to God; and in the second place to establish those who have been reconciled in all holy practice, so that he may present them faultless before the throne of God. Just in proportion as he attains these ends, is his ministry successful. If they are not attained, no matter what else he may have done, his ministry has been a failure. It matters not how much he may have been applauded for eloquence, or how firmly he may have established a reputation for thorough scholarship or accomplished rhetoric, or have acquired rank and position in the denomination to which he belongs, or how large and influential a congregation he may have gathered; if he have neither converted sinners to Christ, nor confirmed saints in holiness, his life, so far as the ministry is concerned, is a blank, on which the Spirit of God has never written a syllable.

But if such be the exclusive object of the ministry, it is interesting to inquire, How may it be attained? The apostle shall answer this question for us: "We have renounced the hidden things of dishonesty, not walking in craftiness, nor handling the word of God deceitfully; but by the manifestation of *the truth* commending ourselves to every man's *conscience* [not his taste or imagination] in the sight of God." But what truth? The truth of Aristotle, or Plato, or Socrates, or truth made known to us by the light of nature? Oh, no! this is not what the apostle termed *the* truth which he manifested to the consciences of men. He had been commissioned to make known the most astonishing truth that had ever fallen on the ears of men: that God had provided for a world justly doomed to eternal death a way of reconciliation, through the death of his well-beloved Son; and that glory, honor, and immortal life were freely offered to every child of Adam who would repent and believe. Compared with this, every other knowledge seemed to him frivolous and contemptible. "I count," said he, "all things but loss for the excellency of the knowledge of Christ Jesus my Lord."

Now this wonderful truth, and all that God has seen fit to make known in connection with it, is contained in the sacred Scriptures. The Saviour, and the men who were inspired by him, have revealed to us in the language of men all that we shall ever know of the unseen world, and of the way in which we shall secure our eternal happiness. God has promised to accompany this truth by the influences of his Holy Spirit, by which alone it can be made effectual to the conversion of men. Hence the duty of the minister of Christ is plain. His object is to convert men. They are to be converted by the manifestation of *the truth of revelation.* There, as I have said, he finds the ideas of God in the language of men. These he presents to the consciences of men. He must do it with plainness, simplicity, and with unshrinking fidelity, knowing not the persons of men, but speaking solemnly in the fear of God. To suppose that he can add to the impressiveness of the word of God, by strengthening it with the reasonings of men, seems to me to be arrant folly. No reason can ever be so strong for any belief as the simple fact that God has said it.

All this, at least, is acknowledged by our universal practice. When we preach we always take, ostensibly as the basis of our discourse, some passage of the word of God. This is called a text; and without it, our communication may be an oration, a speech, a lecture, or an essay, but it is never called a sermon. But why take a text? Simply because we profess in preaching to unfold some idea of inspiration, and, on the authority of God, enforce it on our hearers. If this be not our intention we need no text at all; or we may as well take one from Bacon's Essays or any other work, as from the Scriptures. This being so, it is not enough that we take for our text the words; we must take the *ideas* of the sacred Scriptures. It is not that some idea analogous to that in the text may be found in the Bible; we must endeavor to ascertain the precise idea communicated by the Spirit of God in that particular passage. It is not enough that what we utter may be true; we must, by manifestation of *the* truth revealed to us by

God, commend ourselves to every man's conscience. It is this alone to which the promise of the Holy Spirit is given, and we can ask for his aid in unfolding nothing else.

Hence it is not preaching the gospel to select a phrase of really no moral significance, or the relation of some incidental event, and make this the basis of what we call a sermon. For instance, suppose we take for our text Luke xxiv. 13: "And behold two of them went that same day to a village called Emmaus, which was from Jerusalem about three-score furlongs."

We might begin by a learned discussion on the length of the Jewish furlong; we might compare it with the Roman measures of distance, with the Persian parasang, with the furlong in use among us; and thus determine, with apparent accuracy in miles, rods, and yards, how far Emmaus was from Jerusalem. We might then inquire where this village stood, whether east, west, north, or south from Jerusalem, and inform our audience of all the places now existing which have been taken for this locality, with the reasons which have been adduced in favor of each. If, as might be the case, the preacher himself had visited Jerusalem, he might tell us of the labor he had spent in the personal investigation of this subject; how carefully he had paced the distance between Jerusalem and the various localities which claimed to be the village of Emmaus. He might describe the nature of the soil; the loveliness of a summer morning in Judea; the face of the country; the conversation of his Arab guides, and their incessant call at every turn of the road for additional bucksheesh. Finally, he might return to the point whence he commenced, by confessing that, with all this laborious inquiry, he had been unable to ascertain the locality of Emmaus, and that probably the very foundation of the little village had been erased from the face of the earth. He might close by inquiring who the two disciples were to whom reference is made in the text; imagine their feelings as they ascended the hill that gave them a full view of Jerusalem, and their feelings as they descended it, and the wicked city was hidden from their sight. He might commence the service with a solemn prayer that the truth of God might be made effectual to the conversion of sinners and the edification of saints; the music might be performed with artistic skill; all things be done decently and in order, and the audience dismissed with the apostolic benediction; but, I ask, is not all this trifling with the souls of men? It may all be very proper for an antiquarian lecture; but is it the work of an ambassador of God to men dying in sin, and who must soon, with their preacher, stand before the judgment-seat of Christ?

I have said that the minister should make known to his people the idea conveyed in the text. It is not his business to enter upon the metaphysical doctrines on which it may be supposed to rest, or, leaving the truth made known by the Spirit, to discourse upon the inferences which he may draw from it. For instance, a man might take for his text Luke xiii. 3: "Except ye repent, ye shall all likewise perish."

He might commence with a recital of the various opinions which have been entertained concerning the event which gave rise to this saying of the Saviour. Who were these men whose blood Pilate mingled with their sacrifices; and did this event occur at Jerusalem, or in Galilee; and for what cause was this cruelty inflicted? This naturally leads to the history of Pilate; his appointment as procurator of Judea; his general character for cruelty, meanness, and cupidity; his deposition by Vitellius, and his subsequent death by suicide.

After this introduction, in which really nothing is introduced, the preacher proceeds to the body of his work. He is to discourse about repentance. The subject is important, and it is necessary to commence with first principles. The world is full of *changes*. This important fact he renders impressive by many illustrations drawn from the various appearances of nature. Some changes are for the better, and some for the worse. This admits of copious illustration. Changes in morals are either those of inward principles, or outward practice. The latter follow the former; for if we change our principles, it is natural that we change our practice. This idea is also capable of large amplification, and may lead us into the consideration of the power of motives over the will. Hence the importance, when there is a change of our principles, that it be a change for the better; otherwise it can lead to no good result. Repentance is a change of this kind; it is a sincere regret for the past, with a solemn intention to reform our practice for the future. Such a change is always productive of the best results. To produce such changes temperance societies have been formed, and have been very successful. In fact, it may be remarked generally, that the object of all true reformations is to change the principles of men, and thus amend their practice. This idea is also capable of being very powerfully enforced. If such be the universal law of our being, how great must be the benefit to our souls when the change in question has to do with our relations to God!

The application of these reasonings is evident. We should continually examine our principles of conduct; and if we find them to be wrong, we should change them at once for such as we see to be right, at the same time taking care that there is a corresponding change in our conduct. So, above all, if we find on reflection that the principles which have governed our relations with God are incorrect, we should at once abandon them, and replace them by such as are consistent with his will. Let us do this, and show by our conduct that this change of principles is sincere, and we shall thus escape his displeasure and attain to his favor.

Now if this were clothed in a style of unexceptionable rhetoric, interspersed with illustrations from science and history and the occurrences of every-day life, and delivered with animation and zeal, who doubts that it would pass with a large part of many a congregation for what is called a splendid effort? The style was polished to a hair; the history of Pilate exhibited research; the illustrations, drawn from a large range of knowledge and observation, were apposite; and what could any one ask for more? The sermon may be laid away in a safe place, and become one of the stock-discourses of the author.

But, I ask, in all seriousness, is this preaching the gospel? Must it not require a considerable degree of modest assurance to call together an assembly, many of whom are intelligent men, to listen to the amplification of such a string of truisms? Or, suppose a sinner had come into this assembly asking, "What must I do to be saved?" what word in either of these discourses would have indicated to him the way of salvation? Or, were a man an habitual attendant on just such preaching, how would he ever learn the danger of a life of impenitence, or be taught to flee to Christ for eternal life? When such a preacher and his people stand together at the bar of God, I fear that they must have a most appalling meeting.

How, then, shall a minister of Christ select a text which shall be in truth the foundation of a sermon? He is an ambassador of Christ; and an ambassador is commissioned to make known to those to whom he is sent the precise ideas committed to him by those who have sent him. The minister must do the very same thing. The ideas which God desires him to make known to his fellow-man, are contained in the written word. Let him choose his text, and endeavor to ascertain its meaning by deep meditation and solemn and earnest prayer. I believe that he who seeks the meaning of the word of God with an humble, fervent, and devout desire to know the mind of the Spirit, will rarely wander far from the truth, and will never fall into fatal error. Let him use all the aids in his power; but principally let him read and re-read, looking upward for the illumination of the Holy Spirit, and he will not look in vain. When ministers shall read the Bible a great deal more, and read it with more humble reliance on the teaching of the Spirit, I think we shall have a greatly improved interpretation of the word of God from all our pulpits. I fear that in this respect many of us are greatly deficient.

Let the minister use all the means which God has placed in his power to understand the meaning of the text. Let him then ask, How can this idea of God be made most useful to those whom I am called to address? Let his sermon be the text expanded, and the text the sermon contracted. Let him strive to be the medium of communication between the Spirit of God and his hearers. He is not the servant of man. He is not called to please men, but God. He must preach the preaching that he is bidden, whether men will hear or whether they will forbear. Without doing this, he may accomplish many other things, but without doing this he can never expect the blessing of God upon his labors, nor can he say, when he has finished his course, "I am free from the blood of all men."

But it is hardly enough that a man declare the message of God with clearness and simplicity. This of course is indispensable. But it is to be remembered that he is to declare it to men dead in sin, infatuated with the love of the world, the slaves of their own imaginations, desires, and lusts. They do not love the Sovereign whom he represents, and the language of all their conduct is, "Who is the Lord, that I should obey him?" The mighty God condescends through him to beseech them, and he is commanded to pray them to be reconciled to God. The case, when looked upon in its simple reality, is the most solemn of which the mind can conceive. A company of immortal beings, rapidly approaching the end of their probation, is in danger of eternal death; and we are sent with the good news that a way of escape has been provided, and that the boon of eternal life is offered freely to every one of them. It is of vital importance that they shall believe what we say. But can they believe that we believe it ourselves, unless we put our whole soul into our message, anxious for nothing but their salvation? Simple, honest, affectionate earnestness is of vastly more value than argument.

This leads me to observe that to the preacher of the gospel moral preparation for the pulpit is of far more importance than intellectual, though I fear it is apt to receive far less of our attention. If we satisfy ourselves that we have clearly set forth the truth, we are prone to feel as though our whole work was accomplished. But we may do this without awakening a single emotion, without prompting a single sinner to ask, "What shall I do to be saved?" We handle the most solemn truths too much in a professional way. If we have a well-digested and well-written discourse, we think that is enough. We are all liable to lose sight of the fact that, in a most important sense, we are responsible for the souls of the people committed to our charge.

A soul deeply impressed with a conviction of the infinite holiness of God, a heart touched with tenderness for the men before him who are perishing in sin, and burning with zeal to be the means of saving them from eternal death and bringing them to the cross as trophies of a Saviour's love, constitutes the best preparation for the pulpit. We need the aid of the Spirit of God and the fulfilment of the Saviour's promise, "Lo, I am with you always, even unto the end of the world." But this cannot be attained without a great moral effort; it is the fruit of humble and earnest prayer and deep and holy meditation. In this respect we are, I fear, lamentably deficient. Worldly motives are sufficient to lead us to seek for lucid arrangement, clearness of thought, beauty of style, and all the graces of rhetorical embellishment; but nothing except a present consciousness of love to Christ, and burning zeal for the salvation of men, will furnish us with the right moral preparation. Alas! my brethren, how often do we enter the pulpit with worldly hearts, to urge upon men the danger of worldliness! How often with hard and stony hearts do we preach the necessity of penitence! How often do we urge our brethren to live nearer to God, when we ourselves stand more than they in need of the exhortations which we utter! How often have we spoken of the solemnities of death and judgment, when our conversation, on leaving the house of God, renders it evident that our words have had no effect upon ourselves! Is it, then, any wonder that our preaching has so little effect? What servant of God, upon a review of his ministry, will not confess that this has been his great deficiency, and the sin for which he most needs the forgiveness of God? If we gave as much attention to the preparation of our hearts as to the preparation of our sermons, how different would be the account which we should render at a coming day! Are not many of us in this respect verily guilty of the blood of our brethren? When we all repent and reform, when we never enter the pulpit without a solemn conviction that we are standing between the living and the dead, and when, after every sermon, we can say, in the presence of God, I am clear from the blood of these immortal souls, what a change will be wrought in all our congregations! The people would throng our churches, not to spend an hour pleasantly on the Sabbath day and to listen to music which during the week they had heard at the opera, but because they heard that God was with us of a truth. We should be saved the labor of preaching on the evidences of revelation; for the proof that Christ had ascended, and was shedding abroad that which they saw and heard, would be palpable to every mind. The day of Pentecost would not be an event to be recalled from the depth of twenty centuries, but a visible fact in the present; and, as the prophet foresaw, the windows of heaven would be opened, and a blessing poured out so that there would not be room to receive it.

I conclude this letter with the entreaty that you, and every one who is waiting for the salvation of Israel, will pray for us who minister at the altar, and for the outpouring of the Holy Spirit, that this day may be hastened, and all flesh see the salvation of God.

Yours, truly.

LETTER V.

THE EDIFICATION OF BELIEVERS.

My Dear Brother:

IN my last letter I considered the duty of a minister of Christ as a preacher of repentance. This, however, is but a part of his duty. It belongs to his office to be the means not only of converting sinners, but of establishing saints in the most holy faith. To this other part of his duty let us now direct our attention.

These two departments of service are not, however, so dissimilar as it might at first be supposed. We not unfrequently hear ministers of the gospel spoken of with disparagement, because they do nothing but convert sinners. They are considered as a subordinate class in the ministry; somewhat fanatical; destitute of solid theological learning; unable to build up the church in the knowledge and faith of the gospel. I do not doubt that among those called evangelists there have been many, to whom this description applies, whose only effort is, by the use of all means, within a given time, to collect as many as possible into a church; who go from place to place, awakening a transient excitement, of which the results are far from satisfactory. This is not the kind of preaching which we would recommend. We would have the pastor himself, not the itinerant evangelist, so preach the gospel that by the blessing of God there shall always be many inquiring in earnest what they shall do to be saved, and that every communion season shall welcome to the church a company of recent converts. In a word, I would say that a state of continual revival is the proper and normal condition of a church of Christ. Nothing can more certainly promote its spiritual growth than this moral condition; nothing so much calls into exercise all the graces of the Christian character as beholding the work of God in the conversion of sinners. It calls upon every drowsy Christian to awaken and do again the first works of repentance and faith. It summons the established Christian to new and more self-denying effort, and gives an unwonted reality to the solemn truths of the world to come. It unveils their own hearts to the self-deceived, recalls backsliders from their wanderings, and fills the whole church with the spirit of humility, love, penitence, and zeal. When a church is blessed with frequent conversions, their effects upon the souls of Christians are continually manifesting themselves. Nor are these results merely emotional. Men read their Bibles more; they pray more earnestly for the illumination of the Holy Spirit; they are in the habit of conversing with each other and with unconverted persons on the subject of the soul's salvation; and they cannot live thus without much and deep reflection on the most important doctrines of the gospel. Thus they grow in grace and in the knowledge of our Lord Jesus Christ.

The object of the minister of Christ is not only to convert sinners, but to build up saints in the most holy faith. "Whom we preach," said the apostle, "*warning* every man, and *teaching* every man, in all wisdom, that we may present every man perfect in Christ Jesus." Such should be the object of all the apostle's successors, first to warn, and secondly to teach.

The teaching for the edification of believers may be either doctrinal, experimental, or practical. Let us briefly consider each of them.

A deeper insight into the truths of revelation is the condition by which all spiritual growth is limited. The Scriptures contain the message of the eternal God to every individual of the race of man; and it is of the greatest importance to every individual that he understand it. "All scripture is given by inspiration of God, and is profitable for doctrine, for reproof, for correction, for instruction in righteousness, that the man of God may be perfect, thoroughly furnished unto all good works." To advance this knowledge, is one of the most important ends for which the ministry was instituted. The apostles frequently, and in the most earnest manner, urge upon their converts to increase in the knowledge of God; indeed, they hardly ever press the necessity of growing in grace, without, at the same time, urging the importance of a deeper understanding of the truths of religion. It is evident that a Christian can meditate on divine truth only as he has a knowledge of what it teaches; he can defend religion against its adversaries only as he knows what it is that he has to defend; he cannot be prepared to encounter temptation, persecution and trial, "the day of battle and of war," unless he is furnished with the whole armor provided for him by the Captain of his salvation.

The aim of the minister of Christ should, therefore, be, to make his people first of all acquainted with the great truths of the gospel, and to make these throughout the burden of his message. It is by these alone that the Christian life is maintained. "As new-born babes," says the apostle Peter, "desire the sincere [pure] milk of the word, that ye may grow thereby;" not fanciful human deductions from the word, but the pure, unadulterated word itself. We all know the eminent usefulness of Legh Richmond as a minister of Christ. His biographer informs us that he was often heard to declare "that two great subjects pervaded the Bible — sin and salvation from sin; and that these ought to form the basis of the Christian ministry. In his addresses from the pulpit he never failed to point out, distinctly and forcibly, man's ruin by the fall; his condition under the law, and his moral inability to deliver himself by any power or strength of his own; the divinity and incarnation of the Son of God; free and full justification through faith in the atoning blood and righteousness of the Redeemer; the nature of justifying faith, its fruits and evidences; the agency of the Holy Spirit in the regeneration and sanctification of believers; and the necessity of a renewed heart and of holiness of life, not as a title to heaven, but as a meetness for its enjoyment.

"These doctrines have been the food of the church in all ages, the manna which has sustained her children in the many and diversified scenes of human trial and infirmity; they have been the song of their pilgrimage, their joy in tribulation, their light in darkness, and their guide to life and immortality."

I would ask, Are these topics, and others just like them, presented with sufficient frequency, distinctness, and earnestness to our congregations? Do they form the subject-matter of conversation among Christians? Let us take the evidence furnished by an ordinary conference meeting. A few exhortations to repent, urged in almost the same words by some two or three, and these generally the same persons, form the matter of most of our meetings of this sort. When do we hear private Christians speak of the great doctrines of the gospel as if they were in the habit of reading the Bible and reflecting upon it? At an agricultural meeting men talk freely of agriculture. At a meeting of chemists they talk of chemistry in its various aspects, theoretical and practical. At such meetings men present their views on every matter of interest; they tell their experiences, — what they have done, when they have succeeded, and when they have failed. Why should not Christians, when they come together, act on the same principles?

But it may be said that our hearers all have the Bible in their own language: the world is filled with books needful for the instruction of men in the knowledge of the truths of the word of God: this work may safely be left to Sabbath schools and Bible classes. Is the aid of the minister required to do for the people what they can do for themselves?

In reply to this, it may be asked, What, then, is the need of the ministry at all? If the people can know their duty, and find for themselves the motives for performing it, why not abolish the ministry altogether? If the progress of the age has been so rapid that it is in advance of the ministry, and now, without the ministry, can do what formerly it could only do with it, then has the ministry become valueless, and we may, without loss, dismiss it.

But I suppose a great object of the ministry to be, to lead our hearers to study the Bible for themselves. The minister of Christ is set apart not to deliver his own theories, or to discuss matters merely incidental to the truths of the gospel, but to make known to men the ideas of the living God contained in the Scriptures. His preaching should teach men to understand the Bible better, and to love it more. That minister has nobly accomplished his labor who has been the means of rendering his people earnest, devout, and intelligent students of the Scriptures. As I have said before, in preparing to preach, the minister should ascertain, as far as possible, the very idea communicated by the Spirit in the text which he has chosen. If he have done this, the text will fasten itself upon the mind of the hearer, the sermon will enable him to understand the text, the text will enable him to remember the sermon, and both will be treasured up for spiritual instruction.

But all this benefit is lost when a text is taken merely as a matter of form, simply as a motto, with which the ensuing discourse has no connection; or when some isolated phrase is taken as a text, and a large part of a discourse is employed in showing that an inference may be drawn from it which every one sees to be entirely alien from the obvious scope of the passage. Is it any wonder that men come to consider the Bible unlike any other book, a book of riddles, in which every sentence may be made to mean whatever the preacher pleases, and which no one but the preacher is able to explain? Is it any wonder that Christians lose all confidence in their power to explain for themselves a book which is susceptible of so great a variety of almost opposite interpretations?

And here it may not be inappropriate to ask, Why is it that expository preaching has so entirely died out among us? When ministers had comparatively little theological education, such preaching was very common. It was entirely destitute of theological learning, but it was simple and devout, and in most cases threw some light upon the subject, and, at any rate, generally induced the hearers to examine it for themselves. Now, when eight or ten years are spent in the study of language, and in preparation for the ministry, we very rarely hear anything of the kind. Can it be that after all this study men are unwilling to trust themselves to explain and enforce a paragraph of the word of God? Or is it supposed that this kind of preaching is beneath the dignity of the pulpit, and is to be resigned to Sabbath schools and Bible classes? But I will pursue the subject no further in this direction. Let every minister ask himself whether he has not been deficient in this respect.

The benefits of expository preaching are manifold. In the first place, the particular passage, with its connections, the scope of the thought, with the special force of its individual expressions, are laid open to the mind of the hearer. It will henceforth be a bright spot, which will shine with a clear light in all his subsequent readings. If its practical and experimental lessons have been adequately set forth, he will turn to it with a never-failing interest in the constantly recurring vicissitudes of life. From one such passage he will derive a more distinct knowledge of duty, from another he will learn how to guard against or to resist temptation, and from another he will seek sustaining grace in affliction; and thus his Bible will be studded with gems which he probably would otherwise never have discovered. How many of our congregations at the present day have had their Bibles thus enriched by the expositions of the minister of Christ?

But we may go further. By thus becoming familiar with the manner in which the minister unfolds the word of God, the hearer learns to do it himself. He acquires the power of putting his whole mind into immediate contact with the word of God. He finds that there is an important meaning in every paragraph, and he has faith to believe that he can discover that meaning if he will. He sees it done every Sabbath by another: why should he not do it himself? The Bible ceases to be to him a book of riddles, or of broken, disconnected sentences, but a book which he is confident that God meant him to understand. He prays for the aid of the Holy Spirit; he reads a passage over and over again with the best (and these are commonly the briefest) aids in his power, and, more than all, with the humble and earnest desire to know the whole will of God that he may do it. Following the example of his minister, he seeks for the leading thought of the passage; he seeks for its connection with that which immediately follows; he observes how these bear on the next. He thus gains a knowledge of the direction in which the thought is moving forward. Hence the connection of the several parts with each other becomes obvious. At last, a line of light shines upon this announcement of divine truth by which each portion is made severally luminous, and each casts its light upon every other. He reads and reads again, and at every repetition his soul comes into more intimate communion with the divine idea on which he meditates, until, with Watts, he can say: —

> "And when my spirit drinks her fill
> At some sweet word of thine,
> Not mighty men, who share the spoil,
> Have joys compared with mine."

Is it not worth the effort of a lifetime to produce such an effect as this on immortal souls—souls for whom Christ died? Compare with it the reputation for rhetorical skill, the praise of fine writing, the thanks of gay disciples "in language soft as adulation breathes," for the intellectual treat which they have enjoyed, and how contemptible do they all appear! It is the will of Christ that we should "*feed the church of God*, which he has purchased with his own blood;" and does it not become us to "be about our Master's business"?

The Scriptures abundantly teach us that the carnal mind is enmity against God, not loving to retain God in its knowledge. They also teach us that in regeneration, without which we cannot see the kingdom of God, the affections of the soul are changed, and are set on things above and not on things on the earth. The renewed man has a new object for which he lives: it is Christ who died for him and rose again. The things which once awakened in him the keenest interest have now lost their power to charm him. His paramount desire is not to please himself, nor his fellow-men, but God, who trieth the heart, and who so loved him that he gave his Son for his redemption.

But the heart of the believer is only imperfectly sanctified. Habits which have been the growth of a lifetime are not at once eradicated. Impulses that from infancy have never known restraint, require many an effort before they can yield a cheerful submission to the divine will. Associations tending to evil that are awakened by everything around us, cannot in a moment be annihilated. But all these once cherished or scarcely observed tendencies are now the burden and grief of the renewed soul. His aim is to be perfect, as his Father in heaven is perfect. He knows that if he yield himself to the practice of any sin he cannot be a disciple of Christ. Hence the warfare of which the Scriptures speak, of the flesh against the spirit. Hence the ceaseless conflict which is going on within him, the striving of the new man against the sin that dwelleth in him. His spiritual enemy is ever on the alert to surprise him in an unguarded moment, and pollute his best services with sin. All these enemies of his soul he must resist; nay, all of these he must conquer; for the crown of eternal life is given only to the victor. "To him that *overcometh* will I give to sit with me in my throne, even as I have overcome and am set down with my Father in his throne."

Now, it is obvious that such a life as this must have its own peculiar experiences, and it can attain its object only by the aid to be derived from the teachings of the word of God. The youthful Christian needs to be instructed in the nature of that law to which his whole life is to be subjected, and which is quick and powerful, piercing to the dividing of the soul and spirit. He should be taught its bearing upon all his conduct, whether in thought, or word, or action. He must be instructed in the mode of resisting the first approaches of evil, and of banishing at the outset what seem to be only little sins. If he loses the fervor of his first love and is in danger of turning back into the world, he must be taught the peril of his position and the only way of escape. Or, if he has been overtaken by sin, and is overwhelmed with a consciousness of guilt, he is to be brought in penitence and self-loathing to the cross of Christ, crying out from his inmost soul, "Create in me a clean heart, O God, and take not thy Holy Spirit from me." Nor is this instruction needed alone by the young. Christians of every age need the warnings and cautions of a Christian minister. They all have their sorrows, their joys, their disappointments, depressions, and temptations, each belonging to a different period of life; for this warfare ceases not until death. The truths adapted to each case are treasured up in the word of God for his use, and from them the minister is to draw things both new and old, and to present them in public and in private. On no subjects can a minister discourse with greater profit to his brethren than such as I have here indicated.

Nor is this all. The child of God is living in a world lying in wickedness, in all its aspects adverse to a life of faith. The things that are seen and temporal, its wealth, its power, its pride of life, its sensual pleasures, attract us, and without ceaseless vigilance unto prayer, with humble reliance on the Spirit of God, we shall be led away until our feet, like those of Bunyan's pilgrim, stumble on the dark mountains. These, then, are the various vicissitudes of life which are sent for the trial of our faith, or for the sake of fatherly chastisement. Prosperity is a sore trial to the disciples of our day. The love of riches grows by what it feeds on; and if in the time of Christ it was hard for a rich man to enter into the kingdom of heaven, we fear it is no easier now.

Then the love of his Father in heaven is seen in the removal of these idols, to show him how poor a portion is anything earthly. Sickness, pain, and bereavement are employed for the same blessed purpose. Now, all these varied experiences are sent to us for one definite end, our advancement in holiness. But the Christian will learn thus to esteem them only by contemplating them in the light of the word of God; in reliance on the exceeding great and precious promises. It is the privilege of the minister of Christ to bring these spiritual consolations before his people, to render them skilful in the use of all the weapons of the holy warfare, that they may be beforehand prepared to meet every trial that shall assail them. How blessed is the church that is thus strengthened with might, by the Spirit, in the inner man! When prosperity is sent they receive it with thankfulness, rejoicing that they have more to consecrate to the service of God. When disaster overtakes them, or bereavements crush them to the earth, or trials more bitter than bereavements agitate every feeling of the soul, they know that the hand that presses upon them is the hand of a Father, and say, with Job, "Shall we receive good at the hand of the Lord, and shall we not receive evil?" or, with a greater than Job, "The cup which my Father hath given me, shall I not drink it?" Blessed is the minister who is thus the means of training souls for heaven, and who sees the people of his charge always and everywhere witnesses for Christ. Their outward conduct testifies to the world that religion is a reality, while the inward life, that sustains and governs it, is nourished by the indwelling of the Spirit of God. Cowper's well-known lines exquisitely describe such a relation between a Christian pastor and his people :—

> "By him the violated law speaks out
> Its thunders ; and by him, in strains as sweet
> As angels use, the gospel whispers peace.
> He 'stablishes the strong, restores the weak,
> Reclaims the wanderer, binds the broken heart,
> And, armed himself in panoply complete
> Of heavenly temper, furnishes with arms
> Bright as his own, and trains, by every rule
> Of holy discipline, to glorious war,
> The sacramental host of God's elect."
>
> — TASK, BOOK II.

Intimately connected with this branch of our subject is the distinct and discriminating exhibition of the evidences of Christian character. This will, in part, be accomplished by the experimental preaching of which I have just spoken. When we set forth the dealings of the soul with God, the joys and sorrows, the temptations and deliverances of a religious life, even without reference to the difference between all this and the experiences of the ungodly, we might, perhaps, expect that men would make the application for themselves, and determine whether or not they were regenerate men. Such is manifestly the tendency of such preaching, and hence the proof of its great importance. But so manifold is the deceitfulness of the human heart that men will, if possible, escape the force of any truth that would lead to consequences which they dislike. We must, therefore, come nearer, and so present the evidences of personal piety that no man, if he will give attention to what we say, can possibly mistake them.

What these evidences are I need not specify; they may be found on every page of the New Testament. If religion supposes a total change in the most important moral affections; if in regeneration enmity to God is transformed to filial love; if the love of sin is exchanged for the love of holiness; if self-denial for the good of others assumes the place of selfishness; if the soul is animated with a desire in all things to do the whole will of God; if it is enabled to look with a holy contempt upon all that this world can offer when it stands in competition with the eternal weight of glory, then, surely, there is room enough for such an exhibition of these truths, in contrast with the workings of the unrenewed heart, as shall enable men to discover their moral condition in the sight of God.

That there is need of such preaching, I think is evident from the condition of many of our churches. I fear that of those who make a profession of religion among us, many do not enjoy the comfort of a firm and assured hope resting on a scriptural foundation. Do we not find some whose hope rests upon the fact of their supposed conversion some fifteen or twenty years since; others on their love to the particular church with which they are connected; others on the perfect orthodoxy of their belief; and others on the fact that they would not give up their hope for a thousand worlds? It is unnecessary here to state that none of these is a foundation on which to rest the destinies of an immortal soul. Such persons are, therefore, destitute of one of the greatest blessings: a good hope through grace. I would, however, by no means assert that all such persons are of course destitute of true piety. There may exist in their characters genuine evidences of a renewed mind, which they themselves have never learned to appreciate. Were these faithfully and clearly exhibited, they might attain a well-grounded hope, and their present grounds of reliance would vanish away. But of such persons it is not too much to say that many must be self-deceived. Hence the great importance of urging upon all men the necessity of self-examination, and of teaching them what are the certain evidences of a renewed nature. The true disciple would then find within himself the evidences that he was in the narrow way that leadeth unto life; and, knowing in whom he believed, would grow in grace and become a steadfast and established Christian. The hope of the self-deceived would wither away, and he would be made aware of his danger before it was too late. I know of no preaching that would, with the blessing of God, tend more directly to the building up of Christians in their most holy faith, than that in which this subject is set forth with faithfulness, simplicity, and unfeigned love. Thus when the prophet speaks of an improved condition of religion in the ancient church,—"when they that feared the Lord spake often one to another, and the Lord hearkened and heard it; and a book of remembrance was written before him for them that feared the Lord and that thought upon his name,"—he adds: "Then shall ye return and discern between the righteous and the wicked,—between him that serveth God, and him that serveth him not."

The effect of this sort of preaching upon the irreligious part of a congregation cannot but be beneficial. When the evidences of a renewed and unrenewed soul are plainly set forth, such persons must clearly see that they have no reason to believe themselves children of God. They must be driven to the conclusion that if the religion of the gospel be true, they are in great danger. Their minds are thus open to conviction. The terrors of the law have now a personal application to themselves, and they may thus be led to seek for that which they know they have not, and which has undoubtedly a real existence.

For what reason I know not, this style of preaching has gone almost out of vogue. It seems indeed taken for granted, that every one whose name is recorded on the books of a church has his name also written in the book of life; that all the virgins who went forth to meet the bridegroom were wise; and that the solemn cautions in the Scriptures against self-deception and apostasy, have, for some reason, become useless and inappropriate. It would appear that it is considered in bad taste to suggest that any of the members of the church are in danger, through self-deception or apostasy, of being lost forever. The apostles certainly did not take this view of the subject. The same want of faithfulness is liable to appear in our addresses to the congregation. Who would suppose, from much of our preaching, that there is a large part of every audience unreconciled to God; enemies to him by wicked works, and at this very moment in danger of eternal perdition? The aim of our preaching would seem to be to send every hearer away well pleased; and so to allude to the most solemn realities, that no one should be so far removed from his proprieties as to cry out, Men and brethren, what shall I do? Hence it is not surprising that many a professor of religion quiets himself with the belief that he is as good as his brethren, while those who have made no profession consider themselves not far from the kingdom of heaven; indeed, so near to it that they can step into it at any moment, and that, if they do not, it is no great matter, for that, somehow or other, such persons as they will eventually be saved. I ask, Does not our preaching tend to precisely this result in the congregations of every denomination? I do not mean that such a belief is openly avowed, but does it not commonly exist everywhere around us? Is it, then, a matter of surprise that there are so few conversions among our hearers in middle life; and that such numbers attend the worship of God for a lifetime, and quietly die without having ever had a single solemn, earnest thought of God, of salvation, or the judgment to come? Does this correspond with the apostle's view of the ministry of the gospel: "Now, then, we are ambassadors for Christ; as though God did beseech you by us, we pray you, in Christ's stead, be ye reconciled to God"?

This letter is already too long; but, before I

conclude, I must consider practical religion as a field for the labor of the preacher.

I have long since been convinced that we all greatly err in not preaching with faithfulness and plainness upon the conduct which Christ requires of his disciples. Many of our hearers, and not a few religious men, are guilty of habitual wrongdoing simply from ignorance, an ignorance which should have been dispelled by our teachings from the pulpit.

Christians, as we all know, have been taken out from the world in which all their previous habits have been formed. They once obeyed the commands, and accepted without a question the maxims and precedents, of the society by which they were surrounded. Adjusting their moral standard by the public opinion of their neighbors, their actions gave no alarm to their conscience. When the light of the Holy Spirit shone into their hearts, it first of all displayed to them their sin against God. "Against thee, thee only, have I sinned, and done evil in thy sight." And when the soul submitted to God, it joyfully covenanted to keep all his commandments, as far as it should know them; but of many of the requirements of that law, which is exceeding broad, he must of necessity be ignorant. A blind man restored to sight sees the sun clearly, which he never saw before; but time and instruc-

7

tion are necessary before he will be able to discover and appreciate the ordinary objects of every-day life. So the renewed man, while truly submitting his whole soul to God, may not at first see the application of the moral law to every condition and relation of life. He greatly needs instruction on this subject, and will generally receive it with affectionate gratitude. I know of no means by which a pastor can more surely endear himself to his people, than by teaching them how they may obey the law of God more perfectly.

I will come to particular instances, for thus only can I hope to be understood. How few youthful Christians hesitate to spend a large portion of their time in reading works of fiction, which tend to no other end than to fill the memory with frivolous conceptions, and pictures that allure us towards sin! The book displays talent, it gratifies the love of excitement; and the question whether such a use of time is innocent, or whether it prepares the soul for the indwelling of the Holy Spirit, has never occurred to the thoughtless disciple. How large a portion of the time of Christian people is consumed in fashionable calling, social dissipation, trifling conversation, and attendance upon places of what is called innocent amusement, while they habitually complain that they have small time for reading the Scriptures and private devotion, and none for the meeting for prayer! How few Christians carry their religion into politics, while the great majority vote with their party, without any regard to their allegiance to Christ! How many Christian merchants, having received their mercantile education under an unscrupulous and successful man of the world, have in youth lost their sensibility of conscience, and now, from long habit, daily violate the teachings of the Sermon on the Mount, hardly suspecting that they are doing wrong! How few of the transactions of trade are carried on upon the principles of strict veracity, while men take for their rule the conduct of others to them, instead of the law of the blessed Saviour! How many persons, of whom, in most respects, we think well, are in the habit of large exaggeration! Do Christian men of business know that in the manner and the amount of their gain, and the use which they make of it, they are under the law of Christ, that law delivered to us in the Sermon on the Mount? Do Christian men know that the lust of the flesh, the lust of the eyes, and the pride of life, are, each one, not of the Father, but of the world; and that God gives us prosperity that we may employ it for the promotion of that cause for which his Son became incarnate, and not for the gratification of those desires which offend him and ruin our own souls? The effect of this want of practical knowledge of our duty is most deplorable. The American Board of Commissioners for Foreign Missions, an institution that has no superior in Christendom, and which collects its funds from all the Northern States, does not receive annually as much as is spent in the city of New York for cigars. A small city in New England, of fifty thousand inhabitants, collected in a few days, for bounty to volunteers, as much as the annual receipts of the American Baptist Missionary Union. Does this look as though our brethren of all denominations had been taught the Christian duty of stewardship?

Must there not be something wrong here? Are we in the habit of setting forth, with all plainness, the claims of the law of Christ? Do we not only urge our hearers to be dead to the world, but do we tell them explicitly what being dead to the world means? Who of us has, from the pulpit, instructed his people in the doctrine of veracity, tracing the violations of this law in its most prominent forms, in the house and store and counting-room, and in the various forms of social intercourse? Do not our people, then, sin for want of knowledge? I remember an instance which illustrates my meaning in this respect. A clergyman in a populous town in New England preached a sermon on the text, "Thou shalt not steal."

On Monday morning the streets were all alive with persons carrying back to their owners books, utensils, and every variety of articles which they had borrowed, but which, from carelessness, they had for years neglected to return. They were no sooner reminded of their duty, than they cheerfully hastened to perform it. It is from the want of such preaching that the church of Christ is so sadly conformed to the world. When the conduct of professors of religion cannot be distinguished from that of men of this world, of what use is it for a minister to insist on the necessity of a new birth? How great is the danger of Christians who are living a worldly life! Says Baxter, "How tenderly do we deal with the sins that are so cruelly destroying the souls of our people!"

But it may possibly be asked, Should a minister use personalities in the pulpit? I answer, If he does, he ought never to enter it. To use the office of an ambassador of Christ for the purpose of personal abuse, is shameful and intolerable. This is not needed in order to the faithful discharge of our duty. He may be faithful to Christ without being abusive to men. Chalmers preached his sermons on "The application of the principles of the gospel to mercantile transactions," on Thursdays, to the merchants of Glasgow. His message was delivered with burning earnestness, irresistible power, and unshrinking fidelity; yet, from the beginning to the end of the series, there is not a single shade of personality. Why should we not do so to our people? Many of them sin through ignorance, and would thank us for teaching them their duty more plainly. If any of them know their duty and are violating it for the sake of lucre, or any worldly motive, they specially need that their sin should be plainly set before them. Do we please men or God? Are we moved by the Holy Ghost to soothe men into a slumber from which they will awake only in a lost eternity, or to arouse them from their fatal security, and beseech them to be reconciled to God?

Perhaps I may be allowed to mention a case within my own knowledge, in connection with this subject. At the commencement of the temperance movement, in common with many of my brethren, I preached on the duties of Christians, in reference to this, the sin in question. A day or two afterwards one of the most pious members of my church, who was largely engaged in the wholesale liquor trade, came to see me, and said that if what I had said was true he must relinquish this part of his business. In a short time, at a great pecuniary sacrifice, he did so, and became one of the strongest supporters of the cause of temperance. He remained to the close of his life one of my dearest friends. This individual was the late John Sullivan, of Boston.

But, it may be said, if we preach the gospel of Christ in such simplicity, we shall drive away from our churches the wealthy, the refined, the cultivated, and the intellectual; or, if they remain, they will not be interested in our ministrations. I must say, I doubt it. Cultivated men have a conscience, as well as other men; and it is to the conscience that the truth of the gospel commends itself. By addressing the taste and the imagination instead of the conscience, we throw away at once the great instrument of our power. But grant that all this be so. I ask, are not all souls of equal value? Would a minister preach in Latin because one tenth of his congregation preferred that language, while to nine tenths he would preach in an unknown tongue? The same objection seems to have been made to the preaching of St. Paul at Corinth; and how does he answer it? — "For ye see by our calling, brethren, how that not many wise men after the flesh, not many mighty, not many noble are called; but God hath chosen the foolish things of the world to confound the wise, and God hath chosen the weak things of the world to confound the things that are mighty; and base things of the world, and things that are despised, hath God chosen; yea, and things that are not, to bring to nought things that are, that no flesh should glory in his presence."

I am, yours, truly.

LETTER VI.

MANNER OF PREACHING.

MY DEAR BROTHER:

I HAVE written in my last letter about the *matter* of a minister's preaching. I have now some remarks to make concerning the *manner* of it.

The manner in which the message of the gospel should be communicated is apparent, if we consider the nature of the message and the persons to whom it is addressed. Here is a company of human beings about to enter an eternity in which there can be no change. This short and uncertain life is their only period of probation. The decree must soon go forth, "He that is holy, let him be holy still; and he that is filthy, let him be filthy still." All are sinners against God, and deserving his condemnation. In infinite love he has provided, through the atonement of his Son, a way of pardon and reconciliation, the benefits of which he offers freely to all who will repent and believe. He has sent this man to make known this good news to this people, and to plead with them to accept of it. If they reject it, they sink under the condemnation of the law which they have broken; if they accept it, they rise to glory and everlasting life. Most of this audience are unreconciled to God, liable at every moment to plunge into a lost eternity. Others profess to have embraced the message of salvation; but they are liable to self-deception, and, in a world abounding in temptations, may be seduced into apostasy. Such is the message, and such the condition of the people, whom a minister addresses every time he rises in the pulpit. Was not the question of the apostle appropriate, "Who is sufficient for these things?"

But it is to be observed that this audience is of a very miscellaneous character. They are of every age, from the child in the Sabbath school to its venerable grandparent. There are assembled men and women of every variety of cultivation. A small portion of the audience may be persons of educated and disciplined minds; the greater part belong to the middle walks of life; some are poor; many are young persons, just entering upon the realities of the world, or, if more advanced, are men of active business, of strong common-sense, though destitute of the advantages of literary culture. Great as may be these differences, in one respect they are all on a level: all are tending to the same judgment-seat, and all must hear the announcement, "Come, ye blessed of my Father," or, "Depart, ye cursed, into everlasting fire;" and their final condition depends upon the reception which they give to the message of salvation.

Such being the audience, and such the occasion of his address, it is obvious that the first requisite in the manner of the minister's communication, is, that he be thoroughly understood by every one of his hearers who is of sufficient capacity to comprehend his message.

1. His *words* must be such as all his audience, of ordinary capacity, can understand. The message of salvation was first communicated to men, by the Son of God, in such language that the common people heard him gladly. The gospel may be understood by little children, else what is the use of Sabbath schools? Janeway's "Token for Children" relates many cases of conversion in quite young persons. The daughter of President Edwards gave unequivocal evidences of piety, I think, at the age of four years. In a very interesting revival with which I was acquainted, one of the most interesting converts was an intelligent young person, of eight years of age, who has lately finished her course with joy. We all believe that Sabbath-school teachers should labor for the immediate conversion of their pupils; but this,

of course, supposes it possible that they can make themselves understood. It may be said that these teachers are young persons and imperfectly educated, and it cannot be expected that learned men can render their weighty thoughts comprehensible to children and ignorant men and women. Then, I say, if the effect of learning is to keep men from being understood by the common people, the less we have of it the better. The use of learning is to make these truths perfectly plain; and he who renders it the means of making them obscure, deserves to be esteemed a smatterer and a sham. We may be pretty sure that his learning is little, and his common-sense less.

I say that the *words* used in the pulpit should be such as the whole audience can understand. It is not sufficient that the words can be found in Webster's or Worcester's Dictionary, or that they occur sometimes in magazines and reviews. People do not carry either Webster or Worcester to church with them; nor is the percentage large, in any ordinary congregation, who read magazines and reviews. The words should be, in the main, such as we would use in common conversation with the people whom we address; that is, established and well-known English. In some denominations, the use of abstract theological terms, intended to convey the endless distinctions of the schoolmen, is common. When I say theological, I refer to those terms which have been invented to express the ideas of man, and not the words used in Scripture to express the ideas of God. Whatever may be said to the contrary, I can hardly conceive that a minister can use the language of the Scriptures in the pulpit too freely, provided he use it appropriately and reverently. Let a man read the sermons of Leighton, and Baxter, or Jay, or Payson, if he would learn how greatly familiarity with the language of the Scripture adds to the power of him who addresses his fellow-men on the subject of their salvation.

I remember, nevertheless, that John Foster, a very high authority, attributes the aversion of men of taste to revealed religon, in part, at least, to the irreverent, and frequently ludicrous manner, in which the Scriptures are quoted in the pulpit. There may be, no doubt, a foundation for the censure of the great essayist; though it must be a very slight one, for the preachers whom he condemns, and the persons whom he supposes to be injured by them, do not often come in contact. Be this, however, as it may, the effect of the essay has been, I think, upon the whole, decidedly mischievous. It has led many preachers to suppose that it was out of taste, or indicative of a want of education, or, in fact, decidedly rustic, to quote frequently from the Scriptures. It has led to the belief that the language of the pulpit must have nothing to distinguish it from that of any secular composition, and that a popular article in a review may well serve as a model for the style of a sermon. Hence the style of the pulpit is becoming secular; and frequently, after the reading of the text, you will not hear a Scriptural expression until the final amen, which has not yet been dispensed with. The same paper has not very unfrequently been put to triple duty. It first appears as a sermon, then as a platform address, or as a lecture before some literary society, and then as an article for some popular magazine, to which it may easily be adapted by cutting off the text and omitting a few sentences of the closing paragraph.

It has thus naturally come to the pass, that words are introduced into sermons which a great part of the audience never meet with in their limited reading, or hear used in ordinary conversation. Some of these are derived from the Latin, but a greater part from the German. We hear much of the "objective and subjective," of "standpoints," "of the great problem of human existence," and a variety of other problems. Allusion is frequent to such sciences as Political Economy, Chemistry, Geology, and Astronomy. Each one of these furnishes its addition to the vocabulary of the pulpit, to say nothing of the terms sometimes derived from spiritualism and its kindred delusions. Now all this seems to me unfortunate. If these terms are understood, they bring the message of God into too near a relation to things secular; if not understood, they clothe the whole discourse with mist and obscurity, — it may be a bright mist, but it is a mist notwithstanding. With the vain and frivolous it may give the preacher a reputation for great depth of learning; for men generally consider that to be profound which they do not understand. I ask, Is there any idea on the great subject of man's salvation, is there any idea which the Holy Spirit would have us communicate to men, which cannot be expressed in plain Saxon-English? This is the language which all men understand; and, for plainness and force, it stands unrivalled. Can any man give a sufficient reason why we should not use it in our addresses from the pulpit?

But the *style* of the pulpit, if I apprehend it aright, is also in some respects exceptionable. Improper words occur only occasionally; but style pervades everything. I fear that the tendency of the pulpit is to a style which, in a great measure, fails to accomplish the purpose for which it is intended. It is a written and not a spoken style. It deals with truth in the abstract, and is rather suited to a dissertation than a popular address. The most solemn truths are so indirectly alluded to, that the hearer either fails to comprehend the meaning of the speaker, or else sees it through a glass darkly, and never thinks of it as a matter of personal application. The tendency is to show how things are, and not what we, as individuals, have to do. We sometimes hear an attempt to elucidate some thesis more or less connected with revealed truth,—handsomely written, adorned with figurative language, and illustrated by allusions to the literature of the day, — leaving the hearers to make the application, if indeed there is any application to be made. The sentences are all correctly constructed. The manuscript is prepared for the press, if any are desirous to print it. But its mode of communicating truth is very different from that which men use when they address each other on a subject of practical importance. And what are the hearers doing during its delivery? Within a few minutes after the preacher has commenced, one eye after another begins to gaze on vacancy, the mind has wandered off in some other direction; a large part of the audience has evidently lost the train of thought, if there be a train of thought; watches begin to be pulled out; one after another falls asleep; only here and there is one to be found who has followed the speaker to the close. Nor is this to be wondered at; on the contrary, it is just what might have been expected. The sermon has been composed, not for these men and women and children, but for the author's conception of humanity in the abstract; that is, for a certain being possessed of taste, understanding, and possibly conscience; or, if for the audience addressed, for only one in twenty of them. The one in twenty may have followed the speaker; but it was not designed for the rest, and the rest neither understood nor even heard it.

We frequently hear of the eloquence of Demosthenes. His Philippics were addressed to the public assembly of the citizens of Athens, and have transmitted his name to us with imperishable honor. Yet I do not believe that there was a man in all that vast assembly who did not understand every sentence on the instant that Demosthenes uttered it. Their whole essence is, as it appears to me, plain, simple, concentrated, burning common-sense. We search these discourses in vain for the flowers of rhetoric, for fine writing in any of its forms, for beauty of expression which shall disguise an important truth; but we see everywhere the outpouring of a soul intensely in earnest, which can find utterance in nothing but the most direct appeal, the most pungent questions, and the simplest reasonings from what they all knew and felt, thus coming home to the business and bosom of every man who heard him. No one left that assembly praising Demosthenes for being a fine writer, or an elegant rhetorician; but every man learned that there was something for him to do, and the universal cry arose, "Let us march against Philip." So the sermon which creates in the hearer nothing but admiration of the speaker, is always a failure. That only is a successful sermon which sends every hearer to his closet with the importunate inquiry, "What shall I do to be saved?"

I cannot leave the consideration of the manner of preaching, without expressing the opinion that we have greatly erred in substituting reading from a manuscript for direct, unwritten address. If a dissertation on some religious subject were uttered without notes, the speaker would frequently grow warm in the delivery, and eye meeting eye, he would commonly attract the attention of a portion, at least, of an audience. A mutual sympathy binds men together when they look into each other's faces; it acts and re-acts on both parties; and the speaker instinctively labors to carry the audience along with him. But when an abstract dissertation on some not very interesting topic is deliberately read to an assembly, the eyes of the speaker being riveted to his manuscript, and never meeting those of his audience, the effect upon the hearers must be as small as possible. Now, is not the tendency of much of our preaching towards this absolute negative of all practical effect? Do not our audiences commonly leave the house of God as unconcerned about the great subject of the soul's salvation as they entered it? The conversion of a sinner under a sermon has come to be a very rare occurrence. A few are pleased with the style, a few admire the imagery, a few suppose it to be profound, because they do not understand it; but no one is made to feel himself a sinner against God, and no one asks, "What shall I do to be saved?" And, alas! if he should ask the question, would he find anything in the sermon to answer it?

These two methods of preparation for the pulpit tend to awaken dissimilar states of religious feeling. When we write in a quiet study, we may it is true, and if we believe what we preach we actually do, look up to the Holy Spirit for his guidance and direction. But still the *tendency* is apt to be rather to the intellectual than the moral. In writing we strive to present some doctrine clearly, to express it correctly and rhetorically, and if we have done this to be satisfied. We cannot rise to that feeling of earnestness which enables us to press home the truth which we have presented, directly and affectionately upon the conscience. We feel that we cannot *write* what we know we ought *to say;* at least this, I must confess, has been my own experience. During the preparation of the manuscript there is none of that sensibility of the presence of an audience that makes a preacher tremble in his knees, without which it is said that no one ever spoke well. The sermon is arranged according to the rules, and by this test the writer knows that it is a good one, that the audience *ought* to like it; and with this he is too prone to be content. He enters the pulpit with more or less of this assurance. He has no need to pray for the assistance of the Holy Spirit so far as the matter is concerned, for that is all prepared already. He may pray that it may be received into good hearts, but he has no wish that it be different from what it is. He has no fear of breaking down, if only his voice and eye-sight remain; for it is all plainly written out to a syllable before him. He reads it with such animation as may be natural to him, or with none at all, looking steadily at his manuscript, and rarely or never catching the eyes of his audience. If he makes a gesture, it is with his eyes fixed on his paper; one hand on the line which he is in danger of losing, and the other sawing the air without any kind of significance. When he closes, he perhaps feels that he has not succeeded in arresting the attention of the people. He has labored hard, but the result has not corresponded with the pains that he has taken. Something has been the matter, but he does not know what it is.

On the other hand, let a man know that he is about to address an audience on a subject of infinite importance, looking them directly in the eyes, and speaking as man speaketh to man, with the simple design of leading them at once to some action which shall affect their destinies for eternity. He prayerfully selects a subject which seems best adapted to the wants of his people. Looking for the promised aid of the Holy Spirit, he endeavors to penetrate its meaning, and discover its applications to those whom he is to address. His preparation is a constant intercourse between his spirit and the Spirit of all truth. His object is to say precisely what is given him to say by the Master. The style in which he shall make known the truth gives him no uneasiness, for he is accustomed in conversation to use good English; there is no reason why he should not use it in the pulpit, and that is all that is required. Filled thus with his subject, he comes before his people to deliver his message. As he looks around him, and reflects upon the position which he holds and the consequences which may ensue to his hearers and himself from the service before him, his heart sinks within him, and he not only knows, but feels, that there is no help for him but in God. He pleads the promises, and looks up to the Holy Spirit for aid, casting aside all desire to please men; and, conscious that he has no other intention than to declare the whole counsel of God, he rises to speak. The audience at once perceive that he is deeply in earnest. They look upon him with sympathy, such as nothing but unaffected earnestness can awaken. Their attention inspires him with confidence, and he proceeds in the delivery of his message. Gaining strength as he advances, he feels himself at home before his audience; and when he sits down he is conscious that, to the best of his ability, he has made known the whole counsel of God. He may frequently, at first, be aware of failure, and find that, in the agitation of the moment, the thoughts which he deemed most important escaped from his recollection. But with every attempt the liability of failure diminishes. He acquires the power of thinking on his legs. His trembling, agitated reliance on the Holy Spirit is changed into habitual trustful confidence. He never rises in the pulpit without an earnest, cheerful hope of producing some immediate, practical effect upon his hearers. Nor is he apt to be disappointed. The example of his sincerity and love animates

Christians, and attracts the attention of the careless; for it is not in man not to be affected by that genuine love of souls that shines in the eye and speaks in the tones of a faithful and beseeching ambassador of Christ. The Spirit speaks through him to the hearts of men; saints are established in the faith, and sinners are turned to righteousness.

I, of course, by no means assert that all preachers from manuscript are such as I have referred to in the first example, or that all preachers without notes are such as I have described in the second. I know well that some of our most effective preachers have always used written preparation, and that some of our least useful ministers preach extemporaneously. I speak not of individual cases, and only insist on the tendency of these two modes of preparation. Let it be granted that the promises of the gospel mean anything, and let it be conceded that there is any Holy Spirit, and then let any one compare these two methods of addressing our fellow-men on the subject of their souls' salvation, and decide which is more likely to become a blessing to the minister himself, and which is the more likely to bring a blessing to his hearers.

I know it is frequently said that the subject on which a minister preaches is so important, and it is of so much consequence that men should know the exact truth, that we ought not to trust ourselves to speak from the pulpit without the most carefully written preparation.

But let us not be led astray by words; let us look at realities. Do written sermons always convey sound theology (and by sound theology I mean the simple truth revealed to us by our Saviour and his apostles)? Do men professing the same sentiments as ourselves never read from a manuscript statements of doctrine to which we cannot assent? It is said we need carefully written preparations. But how often do the most of us deliver from the pulpit *carefully written* discourses, except it be at ordinations, or on some other special occasions? A really extemporaneous discourse may be written as well as spoken without writing. A large proportion of our written discourses is prepared in a driving hurry, late on Saturday night, and sometimes between the services on the Sabbath; and the thoughts are huddled together with little arrangement, and less meditation. Is not such a sermon, though *written*, liable to all the objections commonly raised against *extempore* preaching? Nay, if the same time had been spent in earnest thought, would not the discourse have been more carefully prepared than by the simple process of writing? Men seem to suppose that what is written must, of course, be sound sense. I confess I have not always found it so; and I have sometimes been tempted to ask, Would a preacher be willing to look his audience in the face, and utter such common-place truisms as he delivers from a manuscript, looking on his paper?

But it is sometimes said that this power of preaching extempore is a special gift. This can hardly be the case. Those denominations which require extemporaneous preaching find no difficulty in supplying their pulpits with such preachers in abundance.[1] Students in college, in their debating societies, acquire a considerable facility in extempore speaking. Those of them who study law learn to speak extempore as a part of their profession, while those who study for the ministry cannot deliver a discourse of twenty-five or thirty minutes unless every word of it is written and laid before them. Now, what can be the reason of this? When the Holy Ghost calls men to the ministry, does he, by that act, deprive them of the natural power of addressing their fellow-men most effectively? Does the gift of the Holy Spirit deprive men of the power of utterance, and take from them the aptness to teach which they possessed before in common with other men? I know that there are differences in the degree in which

[1] I see it mentioned in the papers that Rev. Dr. Begg has given notice that he will move the Presbytery to adopt means to put an end among the students to the reading of sermons in the Free Church of Scotland.

the power of public speaking is bestowed, but by diligent attention and constant practice it may be acquired by any man who possesses the gifts required for a minister of the gospel. Nay, the men who declare that it cannot be acquired are themselves the strongest proof that on this subject they are in error. Attend any of our ecclesiastical meetings, associations, conventions, presbyteries, annual meetings of missionary organizations, and the very men who cannot *preach* without writing, if a question of interest arises, will speak, with the greatest fluency, for half an hour or more, even without any preparation. What they so readily do in one case, why should they not do in the other?

But we do not apply the same rule to others which we assume for ourselves. We declare it is impossible for *us* to address men from the pulpit on the subject of religion, without writing out all we have to say. We leave the church, and descend to the lecture-room to attend a conference meeting. We expect our private members to address the audience on the very same subjects, but we never expect them to use a manuscript. What should we say, if, when we called upon one of our brethren to speak, he should excuse himself on the ground that he had not anything written? What sort of a conference meeting would we have, if nothing was spoken which had not been written out, and then read after the manner of the pulpit? I fancy that the minister and the readers would very soon constitute the entire audience. Why should we expect our brethren, engaged in the ordinary pursuits of life, to use a manner of addressing an audience which we declare it impossible for us to acquire after eight or ten years of study devoted to preparation for this very duty?

I object to the custom of addressing an audience from a manuscript for several reasons.

In the first place, the tendency of habitually using written preparations is to the formation of a written instead of a spoken style; to cultivate a habit of writing for the press, instead of uttering our thoughts to an audience. We thus form the habit of using abstract terms, speaking of the most important truths in generalities which men only dimly understand, and which no one applies to himself. It is not the language of ordinary thought or ordinary conversation; and it is as if we addressed them in a foreign tongue, which they only imperfectly understand. What the effect of such preaching must be, or rather how small must be its effect, may easily be imagined. The preacher can rarely be deeply interested in it himself; and it cannot be expected that he will interest others.

Every one knows that the power of a speaker over an audience depends, almost entirely, on the tones of emotion. This was what the ancient orator meant when he said that the first and second and third requisite essential to a public speaker was *delivery*. But emotion, though it commence in the bosom of the speaker, is sustained and deepened and rendered more intense by the reciprocal action of the speaker and the audience upon each other. The earnestness of the speaker, shown in the eyes, the gesture, the tones of the voice, arouses the audience to sympathy. Their eyes answer to his eyes; their breathless attention shows that every tone of his voice thrills their bosoms with emotion; their whole expression reacts upon him, and a mutual sympathy binds them together; and he feels that his heart and theirs are beating in unison. Indignation, sarcasm, pity, sorrow, yearning to create in them the same feeling which agitates him, expressed more powerfully in the tones of the voice than in the words which he utters, sway the audience at his will; and at the close it seems as if they all had but one soul, and that the soul of him who has addressed them. Such was the preaching of Whitfield. Garrick, after hearing him, declared that he would give a hundred pounds to be able to utter the simple exclamation Oh! as Whitfield uttered it.

This power of expressing emotion by the tones of the voice, we may remark in passing, cannot be acquired by art. It must arise from the earnest, honest feeling of the speaker, reflected from the audience before him. A man may rehearse his sermon alone; he may determine how this or that passage should be uttered, or what gesture should accompany the utterance; he may do it again and again before a mirror; he may blacken his manuscript with every kind of sign that shall indicate the expression to be given to the words, but it is all a failure. Nature is not so easily deceived. The hearers see that it is all very elaborately prepared, and very accurately delivered; but somehow or other they are not moved, and it all seems like a boy speaking a piece.

To return; it must, I think, be evident, that the tendency of habitual reading is to annihilate the true tones of emotion in a speaker. His eyes and those of the audience never meet. They look up, and all is blank; for he is looking steadfastly on something else. The tendency is for him gradually to subside into a quiet reader, delivering plainly, and without emotion, what he has prepared with care and attention. This is the more common case. If, however, he rises above this, and is of a more earnest character, he acquires a regular tone of apparent emotion, a rise and fall of the voice at stated intervals, in which every sentence is uttered. The important and the unimportant are both pitched on the same key, and set to the same tune. The tones of real emotion have all died out, and nothing remains but sentence after sentence, whether narrative, hortatory, or emotional, beginning, continuing, and ending with the same pauses, inflections, and emphasis, which no feeling of the soul seems really to pervade. To this kind of delivery, I think, reading generally tends, especially in young men; but it is liable to decline, with advancing years, into that which I have just referred to.

I do not, of course, deny that we have frequently eloquent readers. I rejoice to say that I have listened to many myself; though it was frequently the eloquence of high intellectual rather than of moral excitement. Chalmers was a close reader, and never preached without producing great effect. His soul was always on fire, and he threw it wholly into all he either did or said. It was not in his nature to be prosy. Yet a gentleman who was in the habit of hearing him has assured me that his extempore discourses, delivered to operatives in the outskirts of Glasgow, were far more effective, and more truly eloquent, than the sermons which he delivered with so much applause in the Tron Church of that city.

But let us look at this subject from another point of view. Where, but in the pulpit, would written addresses to a popular assembly be tolerated? Were a lawyer to read to a jury a finely written dissertation, bearing as much on the case before them as many of our sermons do on the salvation of the soul, would he not soon put the whole panel to sleep? Were the same mode of address adopted by senators and representatives, would not the member find himself surrounded by nothing but empty benches? And, finally, were this mode adopted in general, would not the days of Erskine, Brougham, Chatham, and Fox, and of Hamilton, Patrick Henry, Webster, Clay, and Preston have passed away forever?

What then can be the reason why this mode of address has become so prevalent throughout a large part of our country? Among the causes may, perhaps, be the following: —

1. A natural fear of failure, or, as it is called, "breaking down," when a young man is called to address a large assembly; especially when he has never been taught to cultivate the art of public speaking.

2. The ambition to be known as a good writer. Those who have spent eight or ten years in preparation, naturally suppose that the effect of this cultivation will be expected. They do not remember that the effect of cultivation may be manifested with far greater power by extempore than by writ-

ten address. The candidate begins to preach from notes, and the habit once formed is fixed for life. He thinks he cannot do otherwise, and so long as he thinks so the thing is impossible.

3. Nor is this all. If a man has attained any estimation as a fine writer, he is liable to be afraid of his own reputation, and he dares not risk it by extempore address. Besides, what has once been carefully written may be used again, whenever the occasion demands it, without the labor of a new preparation. In a few years a man may acquire a large stock of preaching material, which may be repeated from the same pulpit, or be of still greater benefit if he should change his place of settlement. This feeling is not peculiar to a minister. Every one is looking forward to a life of greater ease, and is willing to lessen his burden in the future, of what sort soever it may be.

But, it will probably be asked, would you advise a young man who has had no practice in public speaking to address a large congregation without any written preparation? I reply, I would not advise a young man, who has had little or no practice in preaching, to address such a congregation at all. A few men have a natural gift for public speaking, and come forth at once in possession of the most important elements required for such a service. The most gifted, however, will, I think, be found to be the men who have cultivated their oratorical power most earnestly. But take men with the average rate of ability for this service, and careful attention and abundant practice are necessary to success in this mode of labor. With these, facility in the art may be acquired by any one who has what the apostle demands in a candidate, "aptness to teach." Let such a man determine that he *will acquire* facility in public address, and let him resolutely apply himself to the means needful to secure success, and he will undoubtedly succeed. If, however, he only adopts this method occasionally, and when he has not been able to write, and must say something, and commence with the remark that he is only going *to talk* to the people, he will, of course, fail; and very likely conclude that the gift of speaking, without writing, was never conferred upon him.

But suppose a young man has paid attention to public speaking, I would by no means advise him to seek for a first settlement in a large congregation, or in a populous city, but rather to avoid them. Let him choose a less prominent place, where, exposed to fewer temptations, he may labor in the Master's service, and confirm those habits of heart and mind, and acquire that skill in the performance of the duties of the ministry, which may prepare him for more extended usefulness. It is unwise to

9

place a young and wholly inexperienced minister in a situation sufficiently arduous to task the skill and energy and talent of a man in the full maturity of his strength. A young man placed in such a situation, if he be conscientious and feels the responsibility placed upon him, will probably labor beyond his strength, and come to a premature grave. If he treat his responsibility lightly, he will perform the work of an ambassador professionally, and, ere long, come to an ignominious failure. Let not a young man suppose that, by taking charge of a small church, his talent will be buried and his sphere of usefulness limited. If he does his duty, that church will not continue small. Men of tried piety, good sense, and ministerial qualifications, are ever in demand; and he will soon have the opportunity of selecting his situation. It is, however, far from certain that his selection, if he act wisely, will be any other place than that in which the great Shepherd has first fixed his lot. A settlement in a city is by no means to be coveted. It was well said by the prophet: "Seekest thou great things for thyself? seek them not." A great city is the chosen place for the throne of the prince of this world, where he reigns with almost uncontrolled dominion. There the lust of the flesh, the lust of the eyes, and the pride of life, find everything to stimulate their growth and provide for their gratification. Some men must occupy such places; but they are to be accepted, if accepted at all, as a duty which cannot be escaped, rather than a distinction that is to be coveted. If it be said that Timothy was a minister of the church at Ephesus while a young man, let it be remembered that the epistles to him at Ephesus were written at the close of the apostle's life, when Timothy could have been no longer young; and, also, that he served for many years as an assistant to the apostle, before he was intrusted with the care of an important church.

I cannot conclude these remarks without making a suggestion to those who have the management of our theological seminaries. I make them in no spirit of unkindness. If I know my own heart, I have no other motive than a desire to promote the progress of the Redeemer's kingdom.

I believe that the conviction is rapidly increasing among thoughtful men that the influence of the pulpit is decreasing. By this I do not mean that ministers are not treated well, so far as this world is concerned, but that their preaching is producing less and less influence over the public mind, and that the message of salvation is heard with less and less concern. To this fact some of our most judicious ministers have borne testimony. Since I commenced writing these pages, I happened to fall into conversation on this subject with a friend who has arrived at high distinction as a lawyer and a legislator. I inquired of him, what was the opinion of gentlemen of his profession on the subject of the Christian religion, when they conversed freely with each other in their professional meetings. He replied: "They think religion a very useful thing for promoting the good order of society and reducing the number of policemen, and they are willing to contribute to its support; but that is all. As to its necessity for the salvation of the soul,— or, in fact, as to its importance for anything else than the present life,— they have no belief at all." This was, I know, a candid testimony; and such is coming to be the opinion of a large class of our most respectable citizens. Our arrangements for the worship of God are becoming so expensive that the greater portion of the middling classes, and nearly all the poor, are excluded from our sanctuaries. Under such circumstances, must not the spiritual power of the Christian religion be on the decrease among us? This condition of things is not limited to our country. The complaint of the inefficiency of the ministry is loud in Great Britain.[1]

[1] A writer in Blackwood's Magazine for August boldly declares that sermons have become a hindrance to devotion, and demands that they be dispensed with altogether, and the service on the

And while this is the case, we are living at this time under the full influence of an educated ministry. Every denomination has its seminaries in abundance, supported at great expense. It has been estimated that when the cost of buildings, libraries, salaries, and gratuities of every kind are included, the theological education of a young man costs his denomination from five hundred to one thousand dollars. The professors are learned, able, and pious men. How is it, then, that, with all these means of cultivating our ministry, its power over the people is decreasing? Must there not be something requiring change in our manner of theological education?

In the first place, I would observe, that our system of theological education is unlike that of any other intended to prepare men for the active duties of life. In a law school, every opportunity is given by practice in moot courts, for acquiring facility in the management of cases; and, besides this, every young lawyer *enters an office*, and is employed in making out legal papers, attending courts, looking up decisions, and doing everything that the law will allow, for the purpose of acquiring

Sabbath confined to reading the Scriptures and the prayers. See, also, in the Atlantic Monthly for March, 1860, the article entitled "Is the religious want of the age met?" and the article on "Church-going" in the New Englander for July, 1862.

practical skill in his profession. The medical student, for a few months in the year, attends lectures; but he at the same time visits the hospitals to observe the modes of treatment, and spends the remainder of the year in the office of a regular physician, observing his practice, visiting patients with him, and, whenever it can be done, taking charge of patients himself, that he may become acquainted with the *every-day duties* of his calling. In Normal schools, the pupil attends lectures on the subjects of instruction; but he is called upon daily to put these lectures into practice, and he is required to teach continually, and thus become prepared to teach for himself. On the contrary, our theological students are collected together in large dormitories, where they associate with no others than themselves, and, for three years, read books and attend lectures and recitations, being, in many cases, even discouraged from preaching, unless at the close of their course. Their views of the ministry are formed not from the observation and experience of actual life, but from the conversations of young men with each other. They of necessity enter the ministry with no practical knowledge of its duties; and that they should be ignorant of the best methods of presenting the truth to living men, is only a thing to be expected. Were men in other departments of life to pursue a similar course, must it not lead to inevitable failure?

In the next place, the business of a minister is to address men in public on the most momentous of all subjects. Is it not desirable, then, that he should learn to address assemblies with the greatest possible effect? Ought he not to be a public speaker rather than a public reader? I do not, of course, mean to advise that men should be taught to speak when they have nothing to say. When I use the word *extempore*, I do not suppose that a man is to address an audience of intelligent people without any preparation; or, as some of our older ministers used to boast, that they did not know what text they would take until they entered the pulpit. I would have young men taught not merely the force of the Greek article, the meaning of the aorist, and the difference between the particles: I would have them familiar with the very ideas and spirit of the word of God, thoroughly imbued with the great doctrines of the gospel, as they are revealed by Christ and his apostles, and not as they are announced in systems of theology. I would have them taught, by habitual practice, how to frame a sermon, or how to think out a train of thought. I would have them taught to deliver this without writing, in addresses in the conference room, and in small auditories, under the eye of an instructor, who should, in private, remark their defects in matter and in manner, and thus learn not only to address men in public, but to do it well. If this method were adopted, can there be any reason why our young evangelists should not come from the schools able to instruct and persuade others with the same power that men possess who address them on other subjects? In other words, I would entreat the officers and guardians of our seminaries to give up the ambition of becoming literary centres, and schools of philological and other learning, and confine themselves to the simple object of making men able and useful ministers of the New Testament.

But, after all, what are we discussing but means and modes of operation? I confess that these all might be put into practice, while we should become but little the better. I believe, however, that the changes which I suggest are of importance mainly as they tend to cultivate a deeper tone of piety, and greater earnestness in the work in which we are engaged. This is what we need above everything else, no matter in what way it can be attained. We need more prayer, more reading of the Scriptures for our own spiritual improvement, as well as for public preparation; we need a more exclusive and entire consecration to our work; we need a victory over the world which shall trample under foot its applause, its wealth, its honors and distinctions, and be willing to become great by becoming little in the sight of men. The first thing for a minister of the gospel to attain is conquest over himself; to be perfectly willing for men to say of him what they please; to bear the contradiction of saints and of sinners, if only he can, by preaching the simple truths of the gospel, be the means of converting men to Christ, and saving souls from eternal despair. When he has broken these fetters, and thus becomes a freeman in Christ Jesus, he can enter upon his work with a power of faith, with might in the inner man, which those who consent to bow down to the world, and do merely what those around them are doing, can neither attain to nor understand.

I am, yours, truly.

LETTER VII.

PASTORAL VISITATION.

MY DEAR BROTHER:

I HAVE already considered the duty of a minister as a preacher of the gospel. The Apostle Paul, during his ministry at Ephesus, labored, as he tells us, not only publicly, but "from *house to house*, testifying repentance toward God and faith in our Lord Jesus Christ." In this letter I propose to treat of pastoral visitation.

I fear that the discharge of this part of ministerial duty is growing into some disuse among us. The opinion is becoming more and more prevalent, that it is not a part of our *professional* duty, or one which we are under obligation to perform. I have known a minister encourage a younger brother by informing him that he himself *never* visited his people, and that his people did not now expect it; he did not, however, add, what I believe was the fact, that his ministry had been very unfruitful. I have heard of meetings of ministers where this subject was discussed, and, by common consent, it was considered a drudgery — a thing which must be done to some extent, but which they did as little as possible.

There are, however, ministers who look upon this subject differently. They give themselves earnestly to the work of pastoral visitation, and the result has not been hidden. I could mention brethren, whose names are rarely heralded in public places, who make no demonstrations at public meetings, to whose churches the Lord adds every month of those who shall be saved, while the churches around them, from year to year, hardly maintain their original number. When it is asked, How is it that this brother is so successful in the conversion of souls, and in building up Christians in the faith of the gospel? the answer is somewhat in this wise: He is not a great preacher, he is not an elegant writer, he dazzles his people with no remarkable intellectual efforts; but he is a truly devout and humble man; he gives himself wholly to his work, he preaches the gospel in honest, affectionate simplicity, and he spends a large part of his time *in visiting his people.*

If we attend ordinations, it is not uncommon to hear this subject alluded to, both in the charge to the minister and in that to the people. The candidate is faithfully warned not to be broken off from his studies for the sake of going from house to house, and the people are told that they must not expect it of him. If he does not visit them, they must take it for granted that he is on his knees, studying the word of God, and holding communion with his Saviour on their behalf. He is so much engaged in this holy work that they must not disturb him even by calling upon him. I have heard it triumphantly asked, How can they expect their minister to compose sermons like Massillon's, if he do not consume his whole time in solitary study? All this is as solemnly said, by grave and reverend divines, as if there were really any danger that the candidate would ever preach like Massillon, and as if the people would not know whether their minister had time enough for general reading and social visiting, though he had none to employ in testifying from house to house repentance towards God and faith in our Lord Jesus Christ.

Here, then, is certainly an anomalous case. Here is a man who has been moved by the Holy Ghost to assume the work of converting sinners and cultivating the piety of saints. But this, the most effective part of his work, he declines to perform, and considers unworthy of his professional position. Perishing souls need to be instructed in the way of salvation in private, and many of them actually desire it; and yet he refuses to perform this most important part of his duty. Must not this arise from a very imperfect conception of his office as an ambassador of Christ?

Of the practical importance of this form of ministerial labor, I need not form an argument. Let every one ascertain the truth from his own observation and experience. So far as I have known the events that have led to conversion, I have observed, specially of late, that a much larger number has been led to reflection by private conversation than by public ministrations. I hope it will not be considered inappropriate if I refer to my own experience on this subject. I have always been accustomed to attend the ministry of the gospel, and, in my early youth, the preaching, though excellent, was, as I remember, above my comprehension. My parents, now with God, never attended church in the evening, but assembled their children around them to read the Scriptures, repeat hymns, and hold conversation on the subject of personal religion. I know perfectly well that these services at home made a much deeper impression on my mind than the public services of the sanctuary.

When I was a student in college, I continued to be a regular attendant on the ministry. At this moment I cannot recall a single sermon that I heard during this period. I well remember, however, that a class-mate,[1] a pious and consistent Christian, once called me into his room, and faithfully and affectionately conversed with me on the subject of my soul's salvation. To this day I can never think of this act of Christian love without thankfulness to God and to his servant who thus warned me of my danger. I have never seen him since we parted on commencement-day, but I remember him with a warmth of gratitude which I feel for no other of my college friends.

After leaving college, I entered upon the study of medicine. I was sitting alone one day, in the office of the physician with whom I studied, when a plain man, evidently from the country, entered, to procure some medical advice. After we had sat some time in silence or in conversation upon indifferent subjects, without any introduction, he turned to me and asked, "What is the difference between hope and expectation?" I was taken by surprise, and gave him such an answer as occurred to me,—I presume a very imperfect one. He then answered the question himself. "We may *hope* for a thing," said he, "when we have no definite ground on which our hope rests, and while we are making no effort to secure it; as we hope for fair weather, or for rain. When we *expect* a thing, we

[1] The Rev. William R. Bogardus, a minister of the Dutch Reformed Church; now, I believe, in the State of New Jersey.

at least believe that we have some solid ground on which our expectation rests, and we of course make every effort necessary to secure it." He then added, "I suppose every man *hopes* to be saved at last, whatever may be his life, or how much he may neglect the great salvation. A man, however, never *expects* to enter heaven unless he has some solid reason on which his expectation rests, and he endeavors to live in such a manner that his expectation may be realized." He then made a brief application of the subject to me personally, and shortly afterwards left the office. The interview lasted perhaps half an hour. I have never seen that man since. I never knew even his name, but I never think of him without gratitude and love. If ever I shall be so happy as to enter the gates of the New Jerusalem, I know that I shall meet him there, and shall thank him in better language than I can now command, for his Christian care for the soul of a thoughtless stranger. I was then, as I have always been, in the habit of attending the preaching of the gospel; but I can remember no sermon that ever left on my mind so deep an impression as this half hour's conversation. I presume that many persons who may read these lines may have had similar experiences. I say many; I wish I could say all. It has been too often my unfortunate experience in addressing individuals on the subject of personal religion, to be assured that I was the first person who had ever called their attention to the importance of seeking the salvation of their souls, though many of them had spent their lives in the midst of the professed disciples of Christ.

It is, however, proper that I should explain what I mean by pastoral visitation. I do not mean the calling, at stated times, on the members of a congregation, after the manner of what is called good society, to discuss the temperature of the weather, to ascertain the number of children, to allude to the passing topics of the day, and make one's self generally agreeable. This, indeed, is not without its benefits. It establishes an acquaintance between a pastor and his people, where otherwise they might be almost strangers to each other. Such an acquaintance has considerable influence, as it is said, in keeping a society together. It has some effect in inducing attendance on the worship of the Sabbath, and gives additional interest to what a minister may say in the pulpit. It has, however, its disadvantages. It leads to too many invitations to dinner and to evening company, which, from the relations of the parties, it may be difficult to refuse. Such engagements may often occur on the very evening of a religious meeting, and a minister may be tempted to hurry over his service, or, at any rate, is liable to pass from the solemn worship of God to a scene of engrossing worldliness. People are of course led to inquire, If the minister is in earnest in the first part of the evening, what pleasure can he take in the second, or how can he urge upon his hearers victory over the world, and then unite at once in all the levity and frivolity of a fashionable party?

The visiting to which I refer is a very different thing. In urging the duty of pastoral visitation, I would suggest that a minister should devote a large portion of his time to the duty of private conversation, with every member of his congregation, on the subject of personal religion. In visiting a family for this purpose, I suppose he should endeavor to converse with every individual separately; or, if this be not possible, that he should set before them all the duty of repentance and faith in Christ, and, if there be no special obstacle, that he should close the interview with prayer. Of course there should be in this nothing stiff, formal, severe, or forbidding. The minister is doing nothing but what his relation to his hearers absolutely requires. They have chosen him to take the care of their souls, and use every means in his power to save them from eternal death. They believe in the truths which he preaches, or they would not have chosen him to be their minister. If his labors on the Sabbath have been ineffectual, it is certainly reasonable that he should see them in private, and press upon them individually the truths which they have thus far neglected.

Not only the impenitent, but the believer in Christ frequently needs such personal conversation. How many a child of God, forgotten by the world, bereaved by death of all she held dearest on earth, is pining away in sorrow, depressed and almost broken-hearted, with scarcely a friend from whom she can expect Christian consolation. How cheerful to such a one is the visit of the minister of Christ, who will sympathize in her afflictions, and point her to the only source of true consolation; who will speak to her of the Redeemer who bore the heavy burden of her sins, of the rest that remaineth for the people of God, and of the peaceable fruits of righteousness which affliction bears, on soil that has been watered by the deeds of faith and submission and love! Or there may be Christians who are under peculiar temptations to worldliness, to avarice, sensuality, or ambition, who are in great danger of losing the vitality of religion. How seasonable, at such a time, is a visit from a minister of Christ, who comes to warn them of their danger, to strengthen their faith, to quicken their holy resolution, and unite with them in prayer to Him that is able to save, even to the uttermost! Young Christians frequently stand in great need of personal conversation. They desire to do their duty, but are often in doubt as to the meaning or the extent of our Lord's commands. They are imperfectly acquainted with the true evidences of discipleship; and their comfort and growth in grace can only be promoted by more accurate knowledge on this subject. Difficulties beset them which they never anticipated, and they need to be taught how these difficulties may be overcome. What person can so appropriately aid a young Christian, in all his moral exigencies, as the minister of Christ, who, in the hands of God, was the means of his conversion?

When I speak of visiting a *family*, let it not be supposed that this is the only way in which personal conversation on the subject of religion can be carried on. Men who, during the day, are rarely at home, can be frequently found at leisure in their places of business. In the counting-room, the office, or the shop, we may frequently, without difficulty, call them aside for a few minutes to urge them to attend to the great salvation. We need not detain them long; to do so might seem impertinent and intrusive, imputations which we should by all means avoid. A few earnest and loving words, evidently proceeding from the heart, have thus frequently entered the soul of one who has heard the gospel for a lifetime unmoved. Or we may overtake men in the street, and, while walking with them for a few minutes, with kindness and solemnity deliver to them the message of the loving Saviour. Or in company we may frequently find an opportunity to hold conversation with a thoughtless youth, that, by the blessing of God, may end in his conversion. Let a minister be really in earnest in his work, determined to allow no opportunity to pass unimproved, and he will be surprised to find how often occasions present themselves when he can, without intrusiveness, converse with men on the subject of the great salvation.

We need not fear that men will not allow us thus to treat them, but will rudely repulse the minister who is thus seeking their good. It is hardly in man to treat unkindly any one, especially his own chosen minister, who, with disinterested love, is urging him to prepare for death and eternity. On this subject, I may, perhaps, be permitted to speak from a limited experience. I have been in the habit of private conversation with individuals on the subject of religion ever since I became a minister of Christ. I have conversed with the thoughtless, the frivolous, with men of wealth, with the ambitious, and the profane, but I do not recall the instance in which their subsequent conduct ever discovered that they esteemed me the less for all that I had said. I may, moreover, add, that I do not believe that I have any particular facility for this kind of service, and there is no duty upon the discharge of which I enter with so painful a conviction of my own insufficiency. What I have done, I am sure any one of my brethren may do also.

The advantages pertaining to the kind of visiting which I here recommend, are, in my opinion, manifest. To take the lowest view of the case, it is the most effectual means for keeping a society united. I have said that there are advantages to be derived from simple official visiting, by which the minister cultivates the social acquaintance of his people. It is evident that the more this acquaintance is cultivated, the more unwilling will a people be to leave their minister for another. But if this effect is produced by merely personal acquaintance, how much stronger must be the bond which unites a people to him whose whole conduct exhibits a disinterested love for their souls, and whose habit it is, whenever an opportunity offers, to turn their thoughts from the things which they know to be vanity, to things which make for their everlasting peace. This is the minister whom they desire to see in the hour of sickness, and when on the bed of death. When he visits them on such occasions, he has an advantage over every other man; for the themes on which he must then discourse are those to which he has often called their attention. The affection and reverence in which such a minister of Christ is held, binds every family to him by an indissoluble tie. They may not heed his exhortations, but their consciences bear witness that he has done his duty faithfully, and in love, and that if they are lost, the responsibility will not rest upon him. Knowing him to be a true friend, they will be the more ready to come to him in their various trials and perplexities, and thus there will arise unnumbered opportunities of diffusing among his people the spirit of Christian benignity, and of leading them in the path of Christian uprightness. Such is the unbounded influence of disinterested love. When men need a counsellor, to whom will they as readily apply as to one whom they believe will be moved by no selfish designs, but who, in simplicity of heart, will advise them to that course which he believes to be for their good? To a right-minded man, what situation on earth can compare with such a ministration as this? And let me add, this conception has frequently been realized. Let any one read the life of Legh Richmond, and he will see all this exemplified. While he was very successful in converting souls to Christ, and the unflinching rebuker of wrong, the whole parish loved him as a father, and were guided by his suggestions almost as though he were an angel from heaven.

Besides, if a minister is known to the families of his congregation as specially their religious friend, whose life-work it is to turn them from the vanities of this world to the glories of another, they will not expect his presence in those assemblies where fashionable gayety reigns paramount, and everything tends to forgetfulness of God, of judgment, and eternity. They would feel instinctively that the presence of a heavenly-minded man would be out of harmony with such an occasion. They would rarely ask him to such scenes of amusement, and if he were asked they would decidedly choose that he should decline, as decline he certainly would. Thus, while the kind of visiting which I recommend is of great advantage to the temporal and eternal interests of a congregation, it delivers the pastor from temptations which, in many cases, have been fatal to ministerial usefulness.

The proper discharge of this duty will be of great service to the minister himself. When a man habitually embraces every suitable opportunity for conversation with his people on the topic of religion, he will be in no want of subjects for preaching, especially if he be a devout student of the Scriptures. The trembling anxiety of a convicted sinner; the objections to the doctrines of the cross in one who has just begun to consider religion as a matter of personal importance; the transporting joy of the returning penitent; the tendency to relapse into indifference from the pressure of worldly associations; the earnest strivings of the renewed soul after holiness; the steadfast faith of the assured Christian when in the furnace of affliction, and the triumph of the departing saint who is leaving this world in the glorious hope of immortality, — these, and a multitude of such experiences, will crowd upon the mind of the minister, and suggest appropriate texts for the sermons of the ensuing Sabbath. Nor is this all. As a minister rises to address his people, with a large number of whom he has lately held conversation on the subject of religion, he is under no temptation to speak to them in general terms, which not one in ten will understand; but he almost of course speaks to their personal and particular wants; and in doing this he will meet the wants of nearly every individual of his audience. If a man, then, would preach directly and effectively to his people, let him become familiar with their religious condition. If he is in search of subjects, let him lay aside his books, and go out and hold communion with men on eternal things. The great reason why it is so hard to preach is that the minister spends too much of his time in unprofitable reading and conversation, and when the hour arrives for preparation for the pulpit, the current of his associations runs in an entirely different direction; so that it would be much easier to write a lecture on the books which he has been reading, than to urge men, for Christ's sake, to be reconciled to God.

Nor is the effect upon the audience in such a case to be omitted. As the minister looks upon his hearers with the consciousness that he has before him friends with whose moral condition he is familiar, so they feel that they are looking upon a man with whom they are in full sympathy. He is speaking to them on subjects which have been already matters of free conversation between them. His language, his illustrations, the tones of his voice, are those to which they have become accustomed. The children look upon him as a well-known friend. They can understand him, for he has talked to them on those subjects familiarly at home. Thus is it that an audience is formed that has no parallel in interest. Hearts are open to receive instruction, — the instruction of one whom they venerate and love. What richer field of labor can be desired by one who is in reality, as well as in name, an ambassador of Christ? Is it not worth the effort to strive to render all our congregations such audiences as this?

Again, we hear, quite frequently, sermons about dead churches, lifeless churches; and they are exhorted to become working, active churches. But is not an active, working church one in which every member feels his responsibility to labor personally for the conversion of souls, and for the advancement of the cause of Christ? Is not a torpid or dead church one in which the individual members, Gallio-like, care for none of these things; who suffer year after year to pass away without ever speaking even to an intimate acquaintance of his danger; nay, who, so far as they know, have never been the means of the conversion of a single soul? It is of churches of this latter character that ministers complain; and they tell us that they can do nothing, because their people do not labor for Christ.

But let me ask, in all simplicity, how can a minister expect others to do what he will not do himself? When he fails in his duty, his people will naturally fail also. When a minister is silent on the great salvation everywhere but in the pulpit, his people, having no pulpit, will be silent everywhere. Hence, the members of the church are what we, in our sermons, call dead, — men whose lights, if they have any, are placed under a bushel; whose salt, if it be indeed salt, is utterly without savor. Brethren, let us look this matter in the face. I know it is sometimes asserted that our duty is discharged when we have unfolded to men their duty; that we, like the Pharisees of old, are appointed to lay burdens on the shoulders of others which we are not to lift with one of our fingers. Such is not the teaching of common-sense, nor, above all, of Christ and his apostles. If we do not obey our own teaching, no one else will obey it. If we are not examples to the flock, our teaching will go for nothing. All men will say, if you believed this thing to be so important, you would do it yourselves; but if you neglect it, your preaching is only a professional service, and if your duty is discharged by preaching, ours is discharged by hearing, and thus the account is settled between us.

But it will be said that ministers have no time for all this. If they insist on writing all they utter it *may* be more difficult, but this writing is a self-imposed labor. But, taking this into consideration, is it so overwhelming a labor to write two discourses, of half an hour each, in the course of a week? I confess I am ashamed to hear men who have enjoyed eight or ten years of mental cultivation complain of this, as a labor too great for the human faculties. I have said that to a man who writes his discourses, this visiting *may* be more difficult; but this is by no means certain. A mind filled with the subject on which it acts, thinks rapidly. A man in active sympathy with his people will have small need of writing; he will, after a little practice, prefer to lay his notes aside, and speak to them directly. Or, if he choose to write, it will be from the outgushing of his heart, and he will not be obliged to pause every few minutes, pen in hand, gazing on vacancy, as if that would tell him what to write next.

If, at last, it be said that all this is beneath the dignity of our profession, and that we cannot expect an educated man to spend his time in visiting mechanics in their shops and in sitting down with women engaged in their domestic labor to converse with them on the subject of religion, to this objection I have no reply to offer. Let the objector present his case, in its full force, to him who, on his journey to Galilee, "sat thus on the well," and held a memorable conversation with a woman of Samaria.

I am, yours, truly.

LETTER VIII.

OTHER PASTORAL DUTIES.

My Dear Brother:

IN the preceding letters I have treated of the duties of a minister of Christ somewhat in general. But a minister, in the natural course of events, becomes a pastor. Those duties which come upon him specially in this relation are of great importance. To these let us now direct our attention.

The general duty of a minister is to preach publicly, and from house to house. Here he acts as a herald, an announcer of the good news which the Saviour has sent him forth to publish. But when he undertakes the charge of a particular company of believers, he is styled an elder, an overseer, a pastor, an under shepherd, — all which terms evidently suggest duties in many respects unlike those to which we have thus far referred. Some of these let us now consider.

We learn from the New Testament that whenever sinners were converted in any place, they were collected together and organized into a company which is called a church. This organization is formed for one single and specific purpose, to extend the kingdom of Christ; and this it accomplishes, first by the conversion of sinners, and secondly by the improvement of saints in holiness. I much fear that this object, for which alone a church exists, is strangely forgotten. A chemical society is formed for the purpose of increasing or extending the knowledge of chemistry, and the records of its meetings show what they have done, what laws they have investigated, what discoveries they have made, and what experiments they have carried on. That they have given money to others to promote chemical investigation, is not enough; they must, in order to deserve their name, have done something, both individually and collectively, to advance the object of their organization, and what they have done will appear on their record. How does a church-record show, from month to month, what the individual members, or the church collectively, has been doing for Christ? The church commonly meets once a month to hear what missionaries are *doing* to advance the kingdom of the Redeemer; they are pleased to hear of conversions of sinners, the establishment of out-stations, or new churches, ten thousand miles off; but where is the church that meets statedly to devise new measures for the promotion of religion at home, to inquire where can we open a new Sabbath school, or supply with the preaching of the gospel another out-station, or to hear a report of the good that has been accomplished by our labors in these directions; what has been done to save the perishing all around us; what measure have we taken to bring the thoughtless ones under the influences of the gospel, to check the progress of vice, or build each other up in the most holy faith? Do the records of the doings of our churches contain any such entries as these? Where is the pastor who, at every church meeting, relates to his brethren what he is doing to promote the increase of true religion, what is his success, what are the obstacles in his way, and who calls upon his brethren to aid him in the promotion of that work in which they all profess to be united? Where is the church at the stated meetings of which the elder brethren are heard pointing out to the more recent converts the temptations that are most liable to beset them, and the way in which they may best be overcome, or exhorting each other to beware of the snares of the world, or holding up the crown of eternal life which is in reserve for every one that overcometh? It would seem the most natural thing possible for such doings as these to be recorded in the proceedings of a society having for its sole object the extension and perfecting of religion in the souls of men.

Such I suppose to be the normal condition of a Christian church. Can anything less than this save them from the charge of saying what they do not believe, or professing what they do not practise? But I suppose that the duty of stimulating a church to such labor, and of organizing it in such manner as to give it the greatest efficiency, and directing it to proper spheres of action, must devolve on the shepherd, the pastor, the overseer, the leader of the people. What is everybody's business is nobody's business, and nothing is done. The pastor has given his life to this work, and, that he may do it, is relieved from secular care. It is not enough that he admonish his brethren in general terms, and urge them over and over again to be up and doing, as a living and working church. They will hear all this, and every one wait for the church to go forward; no one will feel any individual obligation to do anything, because he is not the church. I think a pastor who wishes to see his church enlarging itself, and gaining victory over the world and subduing men around it to Christ, must go farther than this. The duty of every Christian to labor for the conversion of souls as the only condition of enjoying healthy piety, if not of possessing piety at all, must be pressed with all simplicity and earnestness, and the lesson brought home to every man's conscience. Let the minister, then, look out suitable places in which, two by two, his brethren may labor among the destitute. Let him, as a gospel overseer, put forth the persons best adapted to the work. If it can be but begun, it will increase. When men see others engaged in such a work, they naturally ask, Why should I not do so myself? and thus the common excuse for doing nothing is taken away. Such, according to the Apostle Paul, was the church at Thessalonica. "Ye were," said he, "examples to all that believe in Macedonia and Achaia; for *from you sounded out* the word of the Lord not only in Macedonia and Achaia, but in every place your faith toward God is spread abroad;" — that is, by their direct efforts the word of God was sent into Macedonia and Achaia; but their example also was the means of widely encouraging others to follow in their footsteps. This is, I suppose, the New Testament idea of a church. Nor are such examples confined wholly to the pages of the New Testament. A remarkable instance of the results of such labor has occurred in our own day. About thirty years since, the Baptist church in Hamburg was constituted, having for its pastor the Rev. J. G. Oncken. At its organization it contained but seven members. Carrying into practice the New Testament idea of a church of Christ, these seven members have increased more than a thousand fold, and have proclaimed the gospel extensively in Prussia, have passed into Denmark and Sweden, and in their onward progress have crossed the borders of the Russian Empire. Let a church, on the contrary, have nothing to rely on but its antiquity, its wealth, its conservatism, the piety of its founders, its polar distance from all excitement and irregularity, and the social position of the members of its society, and, although it may have a very respectable standing with the world, it is recorded in the book that shall one day be opened, A church "having a name that it liveth, and is dead."

Again, discipline is a most important part of the duty of a church of Christ. It was so in primitive times, and required the continual watchfulness of the Apostle of the Gentiles. The reason of this is evident. We admit members to the church who give credible evidence that they have been renewed by the grace of God. The evidence of this is two-fold. In the first place, there is a change of their views and feelings on the subject of religion. This must be made known to us by the persons themselves, for it is something that has transpired within the region of their own consciousness. The second evidence is the effect of this change upon their life and conversation. This latter can only be discovered after a suitable time of trial. In this we are all liable to error. We frequently do not allow sufficient time for this change to manifest itself. We are so much rejoiced to witness conversions, that we can hardly wait long enough to discriminate between the true and the false, the tares and the wheat. It may be an amiable weakness to receive members into the Christian church without sufficient evidence of renewal of heart; but it is still a weakness, and its results are frequently alarming. In an excited state of public feeling, emotions are rapidly transmitted from one to another; and, without any intention to deceive, a change from deep sorrow to exultant joy is liable to be mistaken for a change from sin to holiness. I do not believe that cases of intentional hypocrisy are numerous, though the fact that, in most cases, a man gains something in position by connecting himself with a religious body, gives rise to a temptation in this direction. Owing, however, to the allurements of the present life, many of whom we once hoped well, while maintaining the form of religion, turn back into the world. The love of God in a human soul can hardly maintain its existence except by progress; and progress in piety demands a sustained moral effort. If this effort relaxes, the evil dispositions of the heart at once revive, and the man by his conduct can hardly be distinguished from those who know not God. Thus, in the parable of the ten virgins, five are represented as wise and five as foolish. The Apostles Paul and John make frequent mention of those whom they once esteemed to be disciples, but who had apostatized from the faith.

Now, it is manifest that the moral power of a Christian church depends upon the character which its members exhibit to the world around them. If their conduct is such that they are known and read of all men; if they are examples of purity, disinterestedness, charity, and unsullied honor in their dealings with men; if their manner of living be simple and frugal, that they may have the more to give to him that needeth; if they manifest a determination to obey the will of Christ in all things, and are ever more ready to suffer loss than to do wrong, then such a church becomes a witness for God. Whatever be their social position, they are acknowledged to be a company of holy men; not conformed to the world, but a peculiar people, transformed by the renewing of their minds. Every one sees that while in the world they are not of the world, but are victorious over the temptations by which others are vanquished. When the disciples of Christ maintain such a character before men, the exhortations of a minister of the gospel have a definite signification. When he declares that but two classes of men are recognized in the New Testament, saints and sinners, the evidence is before them. When he urges upon them the necessity of regeneration, or a radical change of moral character, he can point to his brethren and ask, Have not these men a preparation for heaven of which others are destitute? and he knows that their conscience can give but one answer. He has no need to preach sermons in proof of the truth of the gospel history, or to show in the abstract that there is such a thing as religion, for the best of all evidence is before them. Here is a type of character which can have been produced by no earthly influence, for it triumphs over everything earthly; and the fact of its existence can be explained on no other supposition than that religion is a reality, and that these men are what they profess to be — the children of God.

But suppose all this to be reversed. Suppose the members of a church, or even a considerable part of them, are as grasping, avaricious, and oppressive in their dealings as other men; that they spend their gains in sensual indulgence and social dissipation; that with the same mouth they overreach their neighbor and speak to him of their hope of salvation; that they are as greedy of office and as unprincipled politicians as other men; suppose, also, that there are men retained in the church, of manifest irreligion, or even of partially known vice, retained there from fear of displeasing relatives or for the sake of swelling the number of its members; — suppose all this, of what use is it for a minister to urge upon his hearers the necessity of a change of heart? They will reply, Of what use can a change of heart be to us, for we are in fact more honest and charitable and honorable than those whom you call saints, nay, we despise the conduct which we daily see them practise. He must be a man of a somewhat peculiar constitution who can long persist in preaching the gospel in plainness and simplicity under these circumstances. But the minister of such a people will not long preach the gospel in plainness and simplicity. From very shame he will cease to urge the distinctive doctrines of the gospel, and subside into a lecturer on subjects more or less directly connected with religion, subjects that can disquiet the conscience of no one. All parties will like him equally well, and all will slumber on quietly, while minister and hearers are rapidly drawing near to the judgment-seat of Christ. I was very much impressed a few days since by the remark of an eminently pious minister of the gospel. It was to this effect: "The greatest obstacle at present to the progress of religion is the lives of those who profess it!"

It is needless to illustrate at greater length the necessity of discipline in the church of Christ. Without it any church will, in process of time, become both in feeling and practice conformed to the world. It will be a stumbling block to the world, having the name of Christ while it really belongs to his enemies. The salt will have lost its savor, and wherewith shall *it* be salted? By discipline I mean such a care of the members over each other, that deviations from the Christian character shall be arrested at the outset; and if they cannot be arrested by faithful and affectionate advice, that such erring members be excluded from the church. It is only in this manner that a church can be a witness for Christ; by the neglect of discipline it in fact becomes a witness against him. Nor in this is there anything tyrannical or oppressive. The church does not make the law. Christ has made it, and the church does nothing but enforce it upon those who voluntarily come under the obligation to obey it. The precept is, *Withdraw* yourselves from every brother that walketh disorderly; and this they are bound to do, unless they would be partakers of other men's sins. The dealing of the Apostle Paul with the erring member of the church at Corinth should be our example in such cases.

This obligation to keep each other from falling

into sin rests upon every member. But in this work who shall take the lead? Evidently the pastor. He is by appointment and by office the shepherd — the overseer of the flock. He, more than any one else, is acquainted with every member of the church. His word will have more effect than that of any other person. His duty in this respect is acknowledged by all. If he know that a brother is in danger of falling into sin, or if by his practice it is evident that he is declining in the Christian life, he is bound to see such brother strictly in private, and endeavor to bring him to repentance and reformation. In many cases this is all that will be required; and no one will be more thankful to the pastor, who has thus delivered him from the snare of the devil, than the erring brother himself. But there are other cases of a different nature. The brother may have been guilty of conduct that is an offense to the world, and a reproach to the cause of Christ. Private admonition is not enough in such a case. The church, as well as the world, knows of it; and if it does not testify its disapprobation of the sin, it becomes a partaker in it. The pastor must bring such a case before the church for its action. He is an overseer, and he must oversee. He is a leader, and he must take the lead in all measures for maintaining the purity of the church to which he ministers. If, then, he know that any member of the church is, by his conduct, bringing disgrace upon the cause of Christ, it is his duty, at once, privately, to reclaim such a brother, if this be possible; or, if this fail, or the matter is one of public offense, it is his next duty to bring the case before the church, that, after suitable examination, they may take such action as the laws of Christ require. If he does not act thus, he fails in his duty; he is destroying his influence as a minister of the gospel, and he is responsible to his Master for the effect of such an example on the world.

But perhaps it may be said, We appoint a standing committee, and they do all the discipline instead of the church. and the pastor. I would answer, It is easy to appoint such a committee to carry on the discipline of the church; but do they do it? Is there commonly any discipline visible, in a church that thus leaves this duty to a committee? I ask, again, By what right do we appoint such a committee? Have Christ or his apostles ever directed it, or informed us what are to be their duties and what their qualifications? Have we any right to change the organization of the church which Christ has established; and what right have we to take from the pastor and the church the responsibility which Christ has conferred exclusively upon them?

The effect of a standing committee is, I think, to establish a power to govern the church, instead of allowing the church to govern itself; to reduce greatly the interest of the members in the doings of the church; to render its meetings a dry and uninteresting formality, and to bring the discipline almost to a nullity, in which the members feel the smallest possible responsibility, as they have devolved that responsibility upon others. It will, I believe, be a good day for the churches of New England, when they restore the pastor to his proper position, and resume for themselves the responsibility which they have no right to delegate to any others. I well know that the duty of discipline is in many cases distasteful, and therefore every one seeks to avoid the discharge of it. This difficulty is not removed by appointing some one to do for us what we do not like to do ourselves. It is not to be supposed that they will like it better than we, and hence it will not be done at all. This is one of the causes of the depressed condition of religion amongst us. The difference between the professed disciples of Christ and other men is becoming every day less and less obvious, and the Saviour might seem to look almost in vain among his churches for one that is his representative among men. God grant that this tendency may be quickly arrested.

Before closing this letter, I desire to refer to the relation between the church and the congregation; or, as it is commonly termed, the church and the society.

So far as I know, in churches of the Congregationalist and Baptist persuasion in New England, this relation is of the following character: The church is composed of men and women who profess to be renewed by the grace of God, separated from the world, who have consecrated themselves and all they possess to Christ for time and eternity. They, however, have no power whatever over the temporalities of the church. The persons who own pews in the meeting-house form what is called the society, a body corporate by law. These may be members of the church or not; they may be believers or unbelievers, their simple title to membership being that they own a pew. A member of the church cannot, without this qualification, belong to the society. It is conceded that the society owns all the property of the church. They, by vote, decide upon all its expenditures; they fix the salary of the minister; they pay for the music, and in fact govern all the expenditures of the corporation. When the pulpit is vacant, a joint committee is appointed, equally from the church and the society, to select a candidate for the pastorate. Half of this committee may be religious, the other half irreligious men. When they have agreed upon a candidate, and he has preached with acceptance, he is first presented to the church. If they elect him, his name is then presented to the society for their approval. If they coincide with the church, he is considered duly elected; otherwise not. If the church and society, therefore, do not coincide, the action of the church goes for nothing, and another candidate must be presented, who will have the sanction of both the church and the society. The society having thus a negative upon the doings of the church, and the power of determining and paying the minister's salary, it comes to pass that, virtually, the election of a minister is frequently determined by them.

Nor is this all. The wealth and social position of a congregation is generally found, not in the church, but the society. The latter are naturally in favor of expensive houses of worship, of artistic music, and of arrangements that shall indicate rank and affluence. In these expenditures, the church must coincide with them, or lose their coöperation. Expenditures of this kind, once commenced, cannot be reduced, but inevitably increase; and the result is, that the worship of God has become, in most of our cities, so costly that the poor, and even the middling classes, are excluded from attendance on our churches, for it is beyond their means. Is it wonderful that in all our populous places the masses are fast lapsing into infidelity, and that the Sabbath is coming to be regarded as a day devoted to idleness, dissipation, and drunkenness?

Besides, this relation places the minister in an embarrassing position. As I have observed, it is liable to have an effect, probably unperceived by himself, on his preaching. It is not every minister who can fearlessly preach the gospel with unfaltering plainness, when, in so doing, he may give offence to those who provide the greater part of his support. Nay, more; should he utter the simple and uncompromising doctrines of the New Testament, and in so doing displease the "leading members of the society," it is very likely that his own brethren would give him to understand that he had been rather injudicious; and the question would immediately arise, If these families withdraw from us, how are our expenses to be met? It is not necessary to say what must be the tendency of such a relation upon a minister. Its effect upon his family is worthy of a passing notice. The society commonly embraces the richest portion of the congregation, and those most in the habit of social intercourse. The minister and his family will be expected to visit among them; and this, from the nature of the case, will engage the larger portion of their visiting. They naturally desire to live, as far as possible, after the manner of those with whom they associate, and hence are led into unnecessary expenses in houses, furniture, dress, and manner of living. Hence it happens, not unfrequently, that the minister's family is drawn into a style of living above the average of that of the members of his church, though far inferior to that of many of the members of his society, while he himself is pinched and straitened in the effort to maintain it. In the meantime, all the benefit of the example of a minister in favor of plainness and simplicity, and indifference to worldly distinction, is lost; and his children are educated in habits of expensiveness utterly at variance with any provision which it is in his power to make for them.

That all these evils everywhere manifest themselves, I by no means assert. I well know that they do not. I know that, in a multitude of instances, gentlemen of the society leave all that belongs to the religious interests of the congregation to the church, and take pleasure in coöperating with them in every good design. This is specially the case when the church itself is earnestly engaged in the promotion of religion. But that the tendency is in the direction which I have pointed out I sincerely believe; and I think I can hardly be mistaken. I know of a case, at a meeting of the society of a Baptist church a few years since, in which the following facts transpired. The subject of the different powers of the church and society having been under discussion, a leading member of the society remarked "that the society owned the meeting-house, and had unlimited control over it and over the pulpit, and that they had a right to place in that pulpit whomsoever they chose; even," said he, "a catholic priest, if they should so determine." When asked what right, then, had the church in this matter, he replied: "They may choose their minister if they like, but it is for us to say whether he shall occupy the pulpit." Such is the *tendency* of this relation; and the harmony that is spoken of where the relation is acknowledged, is owing to the fact that the church avoids coming into collision with the society, and by so doing yields the points essential to its independence until there is no longer any danger of antagonism. When we permanently intrust power over us to others, with the expectation that it will always be used for our advantage, such expectation is very rarely realized. The caution of the Saviour is eminently wise: "Give not that which is holy to the dogs, neither cast ye your pearls before swine, lest they trample them under their feet, and turn again and rend you." The meaning of this homely Jewish proverb, in the mouth of the Saviour, evidently is, Surrender not the control over the cause of religion into the hands of those who have no personal interest in it. You can gain nothing by it, and it will in the end turn to your disadvantage.

Of the absurdity of such a claim it is needless to speak. A church of Christ is established to propagate certain doctrines, participate in certain ordinances, and perform certain duties which they suppose to be commanded by the Saviour. The ownership of their temporal property, by the decisions of courts of law, must vest in corporators, who are called the society; but this ownership is by no means in fee-simple. It is merely a technical ownership, for the intention of better enabling the church to carry out the purpose for which it was organized, and for no other. It is merely a trusteeship, a holding of property for the sake of accomplishing a particular object. It has no power to act for any other purpose.

If still further we look at the nature of a church of Christ, we shall at once perceive that it is essentially at variance with any such relation. A church of Christ is a company of believers, of sinners renewed in the spirit of their minds, reconciled to God by the sacrifice of his Son, and, through grace, inheritors of eternal life. Such is the idea of a church in the New Testament. Now for the good of their own souls, and the conversion of the souls of others, they, in the fear of God, choose a minister whom they believe best qualified to accomplish these purposes. But here comes forward a company of men, who profess no personal interest in the religion of Christ, who may not even believe it to be true, and declare that this man is not our choice; you cannot, therefore, have him for your minister; and you must choose some one whom we shall select. They might just as well dictate to the church in the choice of deacons, or prescribe what ordinances shall be administered, at what time, and in what manner, or who shall or shall not be admitted to the church. If these principles are carried out to their legitimate result, it is obvious that they are wholly antagonistic to the very ideas on which the church of Christ is established. Our fathers long since foresaw the evils which might arise from this relation, and for a time manfully resisted it. They were unwilling to apply for acts of incorporation, and held their property by trustees of their own choosing. The tide of worldliness, however, rose so high, that every barrier was gradually swept away. They were considered overscrupulous, behind the age; but a result has been reached which has justified their apprehensions.

I need not, however, pursue this subject at greater length. When the attention of thoughtful men is turned to it, I apprehend that they will find it to be of graver importance than they have heretofore supposed.

The question will, of course, arise, Supposing all this to be so, what is to be done? The remedy for these evils is apparent; and if Christian men are willing to apply it, there is no doubt of its efficacy. The support of the ministry, and the expenses attendant upon the worship of God, properly belong to the church itself, and to the church alone. They alone have been taught by the Holy Spirit the value of the soul, and the means most likely to lead to its salvation. It is the distinctive duty of their profession, to consecrate themselves and their substance to the promotion of the kingdom of Christ, and complete the work on earth which he came from heaven to accomplish. They should, then, build their own meeting-houses, support their own minister, and, in a word, pay all the expense required for the decent and proper worship of God. They should be ashamed to ask others to do for them what it is their privilege and duty to do for themselves. Much more should they be ashamed to ask men who have no personal interest in religion to minister to their love of magnificence, while, as a compensation, they surrender to them the control of those arrangements on which the prosperity of the cause of Christ vitally depends.

It will, of course, in the first place, be said, If we pursue this course it will cost the church a great deal more money. There can be no doubt on this subject; it undoubtedly will; and is it not just that it should? There are many congregations in which those who have no personal interest in religion pay more towards its expenses than those who profess themselves to be disciples of Christ. Is not this a shame? and is it wonderful if, under these circumstances, we should lay ourselves open to the charge of professing what we really do not believe? And this reproach is rendered the more pungent from the well-known fact that we profess to have surrendered ourselves and all that we possess to the cause of Christ, and have vowed to live no more to ourselves, but to him. On what principle, then, can we surrender the government of his church to others, for the sake of retaining to ourselves a greater portion of the mammon that perisheth? Do we believe the words of our Saviour, "Except a man *be born again* he cannot *see* the kingdom of God"?

But it will be said, If we alone bear the expenses of the worship of God, we can neither erect splendid and costly meeting-houses, nor adorn our services with such accessories as shall attract men of taste, refinement, and intelligence. Possibly this may be so. But who hath required such expenditure at our hands? Are the souls of the few men of taste, refinement, and intelligence, whom we may attract by our architectural costliness, of any more value than the souls of the hundreds of the poor whom, by these very means, we exclude from our sanctuaries? Is not the expensiveness of the worship of God in our cities one of the reasons why the mass of our people are coming to spend the Sabbath in idleness and criminal indulgence?

But it may be said that taste and imagination are given us by our Creator; and is it not right to gratify them in the worship of God, and thus make them subservient to our spiritual improvement? To this I would reply, when the beautiful is at variance with the useful, good taste requires that the former should always give place to the latter. If a column were ever so beautiful, but totally unable to support a building, would not that taste expose itself to scorn which should insist on placing it where it would inevitably work the destruction of the whole edifice? I ask, When did expensive architecture and splendid ceremonial ever conduce to the true worhip of God under the New Testament dispensation? Have not the ages in which the most costly monuments of ecclesiastical architecture have been reared, been also ages of the deepest spiritual darkness? Again, if the kingdom of Christ is to rely for its existence and extension upon the gratification of taste and imagination, and, in general, on the love of the beautiful, is it not strange that the Son of God, when on earth, did not discover it? Music and architecture and ceremonial have their own effect, but it is not the effect of the Spirit of God, nor is the voice of taste as powerful as the voice of conscience; and it is by the action of the Spirit on the conscience that we expect the world to be converted. I know that by splendid ceremonial we may attract the gay and thoughtless, who go to church as they would go to an opera; but let a house of worship be ever so plain, even like the upper chamber at Jerusalem, *if its attendants be really holy men*, if it be known that the Holy Spirit is in the midst of them, making men new creatures in Christ Jesus, the multitude will come together, you cannot keep them away, and they will begin to cry out, "Men and brethren, what shall we do?" Conscience will compel men of all classes to attend such meetings, and nothing can resist its urgency. They will come, not to display their personal adornment, not to gaze upon stained-glass windows, not to listen to artistic music, but to know what they shall do to be saved.

cal architecture have been reared, been also ages of the deepest spiritual darkness? Again, if the kingdom of Christ is to rely for its existence and extension upon the gratification of taste and imagination, and, in general, on the love of the beautiful, is it not strange that the Son of God, when on earth, did not discover it? Music and architecture and ceremonial have their own effect, but it is not the effect of the Spirit of God, nor is the voice of taste as powerful as the voice of conscience; and it is by the action of the Spirit on the conscience that we expect the world to be converted. I know that by splendid ceremonial we may attract the gay and thoughtless, who go to church as they would go to an opera; but let a house of worship be ever so plain, even like the upper chamber at Jerusalem, *if its attendants be really holy men,* if it be known that the Holy Spirit is in the midst of them, making men new creatures in Christ Jesus, the multitude will come together, you cannot keep them away, and they will begin to cry out, "Men and brethren, what shall we do?" Conscience will compel men of all classes to attend such meetings, and nothing can resist its urgency. They will come, not to display their personal adornment, not to gaze upon stained-glass windows, not to listen to artistic music, but to know what they shall do to be saved.

Let it not be supposed that I mean the slightest disrespect to those gentlemen, and there are many such, who, from disinterested benevolence, have labored earnestly and given largely of their substance to support the institutions of religion. I trust I am incapable of feeling towards them any other sentiments than those of gratitude and respect. They have done for us what we ought to have done for ourselves. They themselves must see that the principles on which the present relation between the church and society rest are capable of great abuse, and though they would not abuse it, there are others who might. We wish to be untrammeled in our labor for their eternal welfare, and I am sure they will not blame us. We pray without ceasing for their salvation, and gladly would we welcome them to fellowship with us. But, so long as they refuse to obey the commands of our common Saviour, they must not take it unkindly if we are unwilling to trust his cause in their hands, when, in so doing, we must also commit it to those who will not use their power as they have done. Rather than do this we are willing to assume the whole expense of worship, because we believe it will be for their spiritual good as well as for our own, and expect from them no other material aid than they voluntarily choose to furnish.

I am, yours, truly.

LETTER IX.

MINISTERIAL EXAMPLE.

My Dear Brother:

WE may congratulate each other that we are approaching the end of this prolonged discussion. I say prolonged, because I supposed at the beginning that forty or fifty pages would afford sufficient space for the accomplishment of my purpose. The subject, however, has seemed to increase in importance as I have pursued it, and has led me into other fields, which, at first, I did not intend to occupy. I have but one topic more to which I shall direct your attention. It is ministerial example. Upon this I now purpose to enter.

The importance of the example of a minister of Christ is obvious to the most casual observer. In the first place, he is evidently under the same responsibilities as other men. We always expect that a man's deportment will not be inconsistent with the occupation which he has chosen, and on which his success in life depends. Especially we think it inexcusable folly for a man to allow himself in any habits which would nullify the effect of all his serious labor. A physician, for instance, holds important relations to the community. We intrust to his decisions the lives of those most dear to us. A right-minded physician cannot act in cases which daily present themselves, without a solemn conviction of the responsibility which rests upon him. In a man thus habitually occupied, we naturally look for a gravity of manner, a thoughtfulness of demeanor, in harmony with the circumstances by which he is surrounded. If he be frivolous and trifling; if we plainly perceive that he cares not a rush whether his patient recover or die, provided his fee be secure; if in the midst of a despairing family he can be jocose and unfeeling; and, still more, if his habitual companions are the gay and thoughtless, who know of no serious business in life, we instinctively recoil from him as one whose deportment is utterly inconsistent with the solemnity of the decisions which he is called upon to make. His pocket may be filled with diplomas from all the schools in America and Europe, but it will avail him nothing. Death-beds are not places for trifling, and he will not be asked to approach them.

Or, take the service to which the ministry of the gospel is likened by the Apostle Paul, that of an ambassador. An ambassador is sent, for instance, to a revolted province with terms of peace and reconciliation; and on the success or failure of his mission the life and property of thousands of his fellow-men depend. Every word that he utters will be watched by his hearers with the most jealous attention; for to misunderstand him may be fatal. Nor are his words alone observed: his actions, his general deportment, the very tones of his voice, are worthy of notice. All men wish to know not only what he says, but, from the manner of his saying it, from his general bearing, they wish to learn what is the real verity. Was he actually sent by the sovereign whom he professes to represent? Is he such a person as would be likely to be commissioned on such an errand? Does he really believe the document which he professes to communicate? Does he act as if his message were of unspeakable importance; as though he in fact believed that his hearers were in imminent peril, and that the words which he addressed to them convey their only hope of salvation?

But, suppose that this ambassador, intrusted with a message of transcendent importance, exhibits no particular interest in the delivery of it: suppose he clothes it in language which not more than one in ten can clearly understand: suppose he only presents it when he is paid for it, and then that he is apparently as desirous of raising for himself a literary reputation as of leading men to accept of it; that his communication having been thus delivered, he seems to think no more about it; that except on particular and set occasions he never alludes to the terms of his embassy, and never of his own motion speaks of it even to his most intimate personal friends; that he enters with his rebellious fellow-citizens into all their amusements, and makes the rule of his conduct, not the precepts of his sovereign, but the customs of the society by which he is surrounded, — suppose all this, would any one believe that his mission was a reality, or that he in the least considered the danger to be such as he declared himself commissioned to make known? Would not the men to whom he was accredited slumber on in security until the time of reconciliation had passed away? Then on whom would the responsibility of their destruction rest?

Now, in the light of the New Testament, the responsibility of a physician, or an ambassador, is a small matter in comparison with that of a minister of Christ. In the one case, the interests only of time are treated of; in the other, the interests of eternity. Every word, nay, every action of him who comes as a messenger of God, may have an important effect upon an immortal soul. Men expect from such a person a deportment in harmony with the grave importance of the message which he delivers. If he be habitually frivolous, jocular, or trifling, it is impossible for his hearers to think him in earnest, or that he believes what, on peril of eternal destruction, he calls upon others to believe. How many a moving discourse has been rendered useless by the conversation of half an hour, after the assembly has been dismissed! The minister has destroyed the effect of his preaching in the company into which he has fallen. They repeat it to others; it is the talk of the whole neighborhood; and thus he succeeds in eradicating every trace of seriousness from minds on which he seemed to have produced some good impression. I have, myself, known of just such cases, in which it came to be the common remark: "When Mr. —— is *in* the pulpit we think he should never come *out;* and when he is *out* we think he should never go *in.*" I well remember an instance of this kind, in my own experience. I had been preaching on a solemn subject on a week-day evening, and the audience seemed more than ordinarily interested. In walking out with one of my hearers, I was guilty of making some trifling remark, the spirit of which was wholly at variance with all that I had been saying. I was immediately impressed with my inconsistency and wrong-doing;

and, though more than thirty years have elapsed since this occurrence, I never think of it without regret, and, I hope, repentance; for that one trifling expression may have wrought permanent injury to an immortal soul.

Discerning men recognize at once the tone of character which befits a minister of the gospel. His daily occupation is to warn men to flee from the wrath to come; to point sinners to the Lamb of God; to visit the sick and dying; and, that he may do these things with success, his mind must be habitually penetrated with these momentous ideas. Such thoughts must surround him with an atmosphere utterly repugnant to trifling amusement and social dissipation. Men of sense expect to see the tone of character which such habitual reflection cannot but create; and when they see it they do it honor. It is true they will often welcome a minister to scenes of gayety, because his presence seems to declare that, in his opinion, it is innocent thus to spend the time of an immortal being. It is, however, a cutting, though unintentional rebuke, when a man given up to the world meets a minister amidst a scene of thoughtless frivolity, and, taking his hand, expresses his pleasure at seeing him; adding, in the blandest of tones, "I hardly expected to meet you here!" Luxurious and expensive entertainments, and most of the forms of public amusement, are inappropriate places for him who teaches men "to turn from these vanities to serve the living God." It is not enough to ask, What is the positive harm of these amusements? it is sufficient to say that they constitute one of the gods which men of this world worship, and by which they are led captive by thousands, to their eternal undoing. Nor is this all. It is impossible for hearers to believe that a minister who is seen amidst scenes of fashion and dissipation, is in earnest when he urges them to flee from the wrath to come. If he does not enjoy them, say they, why is he here? If he does enjoy them, say what he will, he is at heart just like one of us. The effect of such associations on a minister's preaching is obvious. That man must be endowed with an unusual amount of modest assurance, who during the week will unite in the gayety of fashionable life, and on the Sabbath preach on the realities of eternity and the absolute necessity of setting our affections on things above, not on things on the earth. An eminent minister of the gospel, the most eloquent preacher that I ever heard, once said to me, "When I was settled in the city of ——, a large number of the most distinguished men in the State attended my church; they were really very kind to me, and always invited me to their dinner-parties. For a while I accepted their invitations. They were men of high intelligence, and their parties were disgraced by no intemperance or excess. But I found that if I dined with them on Saturday I could not preach to the sinners as I wanted to on Sunday; so I broke it off altogether." Did he not, in this case, act as became a minister of reconciliation?

But it will, perhaps, be said that Jesus Christ, when on the earth, accepted invitations to dine, in all companies; and it was even said of him, by way of reproach, "This man receiveth sinners, and eateth with them": why may we not safely take him for our example? Undoubtedly we may, if we will honestly take him as our example. It is true, Jesus Christ seems to have gone into any company to which he was invited, but he always went as a simple preacher of righteousness; and some of the most solemn and searching appeals that he ever delivered were spoken on such occasions. He was with the men around him, but he was not of them; and, setting aside all conventionalities, he employed such occasions, as he did all others, as opportunities for preaching the kingdom of God. If a man will act as Jesus Christ acted, there can be no objection to his going anywhere. If, however, he cannot do this, he had better keep out of the way of temptation. It is certainly innocent for him to stay at home; it is not innocent to go where, by his conduct, he may deny his Master, bring guilt upon his own soul, and place a stumbling-block before the souls of others. William Allen and Stephen Grellet, distinguished members of the Society of Friends, made several journeys on the continent of Europe, on religious missions. They were commonly received with much attention by men of the very highest rank, on account of their personal character and active philanthropy. They were frequently invited to dine with persons eminent for position, with princes, ministers of state, and others of great consideration, and they frequently accepted the invitations. They always, however, went as the disciples of Christ, and entered into no conversation inconsistent with that character; and it was their habit, before the company separated, to spend a portion of time in religious exhortation and prayer. On such, as on all other occasions, it became evident that the object to which every other was subordinate was, to relieve distress, to succor the unfortunate, to circulate the Scriptures, and urge all men to serious attention to the subject of personal religion. Their conduct was thus consistent with their profession, and their addresses were always received with respect, and frequently with thankfulness and tears. Oh that we had many such tourists, both laymen and ministers of the gospel, travelling over Europe at the present day!

Again, no one who has been in the habit of conversation with young persons on the subject of religion, can have failed to observe that the love of social amusement, more than anything else, takes off the thoughts from God and eternity, renders the mind the slave of the things that perish, and presents one of the strongest obstacles to repentance. How can a minister, whose business it is to win souls, sanction, by his presence, amusements which he knows stand directly in the way of a sinner's conversion? It may be said, perhaps, Tell us, then, what are the amusements which a minister may properly attend, and what those which he should avoid? This is not possible, nor is it needful. A sanctified heart will guide a minister aright; to an unsanctified heart rules are of no value. When such a question arises, let him ask himself, in the first place, Is this amusement innocent? in the next place, Is it a suitable occupation for the soul of an immortal being; will it improve my physical, intellectual, or moral health; is it liable to be misunderstood, so that it may be a stumbling-block to others; will it promote or retard the great object to which I have consecrated my life? The answer to these questions will enable a minister to decide correctly, if he really wishes to know the will of the Master. "If meat," says St. Paul, "maketh my brother to offend, I will eat no meat while the world standeth!"

But a minister of the gospel may destroy his power for good directly, as well as indirectly. His special character is that of a moral teacher; and we all know that the power of a moral teacher is measured, in a great degree, by his obedience to the truth which he delivers to others. He may bind as many burdens as he pleases upon the shoulders of other men, but they will easily cast them off if he assume none of them himself. What effect can be produced by an habitual drunkard lecturing on intemperance; or a grasping miser discoursing on charity; or a profligate debauchee setting forth the praises of purity? We must make it evident that we abhor the sins which we denounce, and strive after the excellences which we inculcate, or our teachings will be not merely powerless, they will be odious and offensive.

But to illustrate my meaning by example. The minister of the gospel teaches the vanity of everything earthly and temporal, in comparison with those things eternal in the heavens; but his preaching will be powerless, if, practically, he sets the same value upon things sublunary as those who profess to be living for this world alone. He may preach on the dangers of wealth, and how hard it is for a rich man to enter the kingdom of heaven, but his preaching will avail little if he is as grasping at a bargain, as eager to accumulate, as ready to move in any direction at the offer of a larger salary, as men who profess to be governed by nothing but the love of gain. He may discourse forcibly on the corrupting influence of place and power and station, but it will all be useless if it is observed that he is himself eager after positions of ecclesiastical influence, never tired of hearing his own voice at public meetings, striving to hold the first place among his brethren, coveting literary reputation, academical distinctions, and things which sensible men would be ashamed to aspire after. He may preach most movingly on the universal duty of consecrating all that we possess to the service of Christ, but it will come home to no one's conscience if it be observed that he habitually pleads his office as a reason why he should escape the ordinary sacrifices demanded of his brethren. He may powerfully insist upon making everything subsidiary to the great life-work of saving souls, and may show that we have no right to spend an hour of our time or a dollar of our money without asking whether we have the permission of the Master; but the effect of this preaching will be small if, no matter what is the condition of his parish, he always has leisure for a journey of pleasure, a trip to Europe, or a visit to a watering-place. He may discourse with great soundness of judgment on the duty of Christian parents to bring up their children in the nurture of the Lord, but it will be all labor in vain if he allows his family in every indulgence which his means will any way admit, and if it be observed that he is far more anxious to see them rich, powerful, and applauded, than humble, devout, pious, and self-denying. When such inconsistencies exist, the people hear his words, and look upon his example; they may obey the one, or follow the other. Which will they choose? I need not answer the question. The religious character of a people whose minister preaches the truth ever so eloquently from the pulpit, but whose conduct out of the pulpit is at direct variance with all that he inculcates, will furnish all the reply that is necessary.

I am, yours, truly.

LETTER X.

PERSONAL EXPLANATION.—CONCLUSION.

MY DEAR BROTHER:

WERE I writing for you alone, I should consider my task completed. But as you requested me to write for the public, and as these pages may meet other eyes than yours, a few words, at the close, not for you, but for others, seem to me to be almost indispensable. At any rate, I feel it due to myself to add some suggestions which I have reserved for the close, as they can be more appropriately introduced here than in any other place.

It will very naturally be asked, Were you yourself ever such a minister as you urge us to be? You tell us that our lives must illustrate our teaching. Was your practice such as your teaching prescribes?

I might, perhaps, suggest that this is a matter, not of individual, but of universal concernment. The true question is, Do these evils exist, and ought they to be removed; and not whether they lie at the door of any particular individual. I might have easily avoided this question by publishing what I have written anonymously; but I chose not to do it. I preferred to publish under my own name, and bear to the full whatever odium may attach to making known what I consider to be important truths. If I have not lived as it becomes a Christian minister, I deserve to be blamed for it as much as any of my brethren; and I would humbly bear the rebuke to which my conduct justly exposes me.

If I am asked how I discharged my duty as a pastor, the question is susceptible of two distinct answers: the first from the people to whom I ministered, and the second from my own consciousness in the sight of God. The portion of my life devoted directly to pastoral duty is not large. I was for five years pastor of the First Baptist Church in Boston. So far as the eye of man can discover, they know my walk and conversation. Of those to whom I then ministered the greater part have fallen asleep; but enough of them remain at this present to testify in what respects I did or did not perform my duties as pastor among them; and I know of no reason why they should not testify truly. I think they will bear witness, at least, that I left them a happy, harmonious, and loving band of Christian disciples, and such they have remained until the present day. Of the extent and depth of their attachment to me I had no conception until I had promised to enter another sphere of labor. Had I known of it sooner, I should probably have been their pastor to-day.

Turning away, however, from man's opinion of my pastorate, and reviewing it in the sight of a holy and omniscient God, I must humble myself in the dust, as one of his most unprofitable servants. I do not accuse myself of indolence, or a disposition to shrink from any labor that came upon me as a pastor. I was moved to action by a feeling of responsibility and by a dogged sense of duty that carried me through my work when my health was feeble, and, to many persons, seemed declining. It was not in the amount, but in the kind of labor that I was greatly deficient. Circumstances which it would be needless to mention excited in me an ambition for scholarship and literary reputation. Thus, though I hope I avoided trifling in the pulpit, my preparation for the Sabbath came to be more of an intellectual than a moral exercise. In the mean time my brethren assigned me important duties in connection with missions and education, which soon demanded a large portion of my time. While I was thus continually occupied, my labor tended to draw me away from my own heart, and from effort for the spiritual good of my people. I had little time for reading the word of God and cultivating devout communion with my Saviour. My mind became secularized, and I wandered far from God. When I think how unfaithfully I did the work of an ambassador of Christ, and how far I departed from him, I wonder at the compassion that bore with me, and condescended to give me any, even the least, success.

During the latter part of my ministry, I was painfully conscious of my condition, and was thoroughly dissatisfied with myself. I had, before God, undertaken the care of the souls of my people, and this was the only ground on which I received from them my support. They had a right to my whole time, and I gave them but a part of it; by far the greater part was given to business, which, though relating to the affairs of our denomination, had nothing to do with their spiritual welfare. I saw that, without I gave up everything but my pastoral duty, I could not act justly to my people; but how to do this I did not see possible. Under these circumstances, I accepted a position in a college, with the expectation of soon returning to the ministry, to commence it under different auspices. This expectation was not, however, to be realized. I was soon called to another service in the work of education, which I occupied for nearly thirty years.

In thus exchanging the ministry for the work of education, though I acted with the sanction of all my brethren, I think I erred. It was wrong to place anything in comparison with the work of saving souls. Had I been more solemnly devoted to the labor to which the Master appointed me, I should have escaped this error. During my ministry in Boston, I contracted the habit of writing and reading my sermons. Though I did this at the suggestion of my people, I consider it as one of the great errors of my life. This error I should have escaped if I had thought more of moral preparation for the pulpit, if my mind had been more habitually devout, and I had cultivated a more humble reliance on the Spirit of God. But why should I recall the incidents of a life full of mistakes and moral imperfections? It may, perhaps, be sufficient to say, that, if I have any knowledge of the faults of the ministry, the germs, at least, of that knowledge have been derived from my own painful experience.

When, a few years since, I was called temporarily to the exercise of the pastoral office, I endeavored in some measure to obey the precepts which I have here inculcated upon others. I at once laid aside every other labor, and confined my reading almost exclusively to the Bible and to works on devotional or practical religion. To the measure of my physical ability, I preached the gospel, both publicly and from house to house, seeking to hold personal conversation on the subject of religon, as far as it was possible, with every member of the whole congregation. The Lord in mercy gave me such success as seemed good to him; and though my imperfections were many and my practice fell very far short of my duty as a minister, I can truly say that no part of my ministerial life was so full of enjoyment as this, and upon no part of it do I look back with so much satisfaction. I do firmly believe that, to gain victory over one's self, over the love of reputation, position, or emolument, to consider all things but loss for the excellency of the knowledge of Christ Jesus our Lord, and in the face of all men to preach simply what the word of God teaches, to preach that only, and to do this day after day, no matter what men may think of us, is the only way to secure a happy and successful ministry, to be joyful in our own souls, from the presence of Christ abiding in us, and at last to hear his voice, "Well done, good and faithful servant, enter thou into the joy of thy Lord!"

And now, having made my confession, and placed myself in the condition of the most erring of my brethren, accepting the rebukes which my faults as a minister deserve, I may, with the greater boldness, make my final appeal to the ambassadors of Christ. I pray God that I may write every word in his fear, and if in anything I violate the spirit of Christian love, I may find mercy in the day when the secrets of all hearts shall be made manifest.

We are, in this country, living at a period in which every external obstacle to the progress of religion has been removed. Liberty of speech and of the press is inviolate. Men speak and write their opinions, on all subjects, with unrestrained boldness. There is nothing to prevent us from discipling the whole nation to Christ. The Bible is open to all, and efforts are incessant to furnish every family in our land with a copy of it. The State is sparing neither labor nor expense to enable every child born among us to read it. The sum annually spent for the maintenance of external worship is very great. Magnificent churches are erected in our cities and villages, and the amounts required for carrying on very expensive accessories to worship are liberally provided. Seminaries, which gratuitously furnish a costly education to all, and, in some cases, board and lodging to the indigent, are established by every denomination of Christians. Never before had Christianity so fair an opportunity to subdue all things to obedience to Christ as in these United States. Besides all this, this is, in a special manner, a land of Sabbaths. One day in seven is set apart for the worship of God, and this day ministers have all to themselves. They may occupy as much of this time as they please in making known to us our duty to God and our neighbor, as it has been revealed to us by our Lord and Saviour Jesus Christ. It would seem that we must be a very religious, and, of course, a very moral people, well acquainted with the oracles of God, and thoroughly inclined to reduce them to practice.

And now, what is the actual result of all this? What is the spectacle which this nation at this moment presents to the world! A million or more of our citizens are engaged in mutual slaughter! Hundreds of thousands have already fallen by the sword and by the diseases incident to camps. Of this million of men the greater part have been hearers of the gospel; and all this sacrifice has been rendered necessary in order to maintain the best government that God has ever bestowed upon man.

Again, in this country, intelligence is more widely diffused than in any nation on earth. We choose our own rulers; we are the sovereigns in whom rests exclusively the appointing power. If our public officers are not good men, we have no one to blame but ourselves. If the professors of religion chose to act on the principles of their Master, and consider citizenship as a responsibility for which they must give account, they would easily, without any formal organization, control this nation. But what do we find to be the fact? The people, as is always the case in free governments, are divided into two parties; but that political party is yet to arise which will not sacrifice right to what it considers expediency, and which will not tolerate any wrong when it is supposed that the interests of the party require it. Yet, in the ranks of one or other of these parties religious men are found by the wholesale, aiding and abetting what they know to be wrong, if they suppose it will ensure a majority of votes at the coming election; a majority of votes, perhaps, to be given to a man who has no single moral attribute to entitle him to a suffrage. Thus is the religious influence of the professors of religion reduced to nothing. The maxim seems to be adopted — religion is one thing, and politics another; as though men could carve out a portion of their lives over which God should have no control, and which he would never bring into judgment. And what is the result? The most sagacious observer that ever visited this country was profoundly astonished to see how large was the number of able men *out* of office, and how small was the number in office. But we need not the testimony of foreigners on this subject. Enter the halls of our national legislature, and who is not sick at heart while reflecting that into such hands the destinies of this country have been committed? Has not Washington become the theatre for the display of the most odious of human passions, the chosen seat of corruption, intemperance, and venality? And all this is done under the full light of the pure gospel of Jesus Christ. For this the professors of religion are, at the bar of God, greatly responsible.

Again, observe the flood of intemperance that deluges the land, sweeping away men in every position of life, bringing disgrace upon our public counsels, and hurrying the masses by hundreds of thousands to an untimely grave. It is in the power of the followers of Christ, by wise and just legislation, but especially by precept and example, to arrest this evil. But it is not arrested. We make a movement in this direction every few years, when some political end is to be secured, but when this occasion passes away it is all over. Are Christians, in this matter, the salt of the earth?

Again, the common maxims of trade are confessed to be very unlike the laws of Christ; indeed, so unlike as to be utterly at variance with them. But do Christian men of business so obey the laws of Christ that they form a class by themselves, turning with abhorrence from everything false or dishonest or treacherous or mean? Or do they assimilate themselves with the men about them, under the plea that unless they do as others do they can never grow rich? And after they have grown rich, what is the difference in the manner of expenditure of wealth between him who professes to fear God and him who fears him not? Do not both bow down to the same idols, and sacrifice without stint to sensuality, luxury, and ostentation? I might extend to almost any length this catalogue of our national sins by reference to the vices which we annually import from the licentious capitals of Europe. But the subject is too painful. I forbear.

The question that arises here is, Who is to blame for all this? Can we escape the conclusion that a large share of it rests upon ourselves? Have we, as ambassadors of Christ, made known to men, in all plainness, earnestness, and solemnity, the law of God in all its exceeding broadness? Have we brought this law home to men's business and bosoms, that they might see clearly wherein they have violated it; or have we weakly forborne to tell the truth for fear of giving offence? Have we made known this law with all its tremendous sanctions, or have we so glozed over the truth that no one would from our preaching suppose that he was in any particular danger? Have we clearly discerned between the righteous and the wicked, or have we taken it for granted that every one who says, Lord! Lord! shall enter into the kingdom of heaven? Have we, with all plainness, delivered "the message which we have heard from him, that God is light, and in him there is no darkness at all;" and "that if we say that we have fellowship with him and walk in darkness, we lie, and do not the truth"? Have we preached clearly that, no matter what may be our experiences, "this is the love of God, that we keep his commandments"? Have we impressed it upon men that our hope of heaven is all a fallacy unless we are ready to obey Christ in *all* things, though it cost us the surrender of human applause, the riches of the world, and expose us to persecution, reproach, nay, death itself; and do we thus obey him? Have we not all sinned in this respect, and become guilty of our brother's blood? I confess, with shame, that in all these things I have greatly failed in my duty. Is it not so with you?

If the awful chastisement which is now laid upon our country for our sins is in any respect owing to our unfaithfulness, how great must be our guilt, and how fearful our responsibility! Words are inadequate to express the solemnity of our position. Let each one apply the oracles of God honestly to his own conscience, and he will feel what words cannot utter.

What, then, is to be done? The past cannot be recalled. The results of our unfaithfulness have, for the most part, passed before us into eternity. The present is still with us, and now is the day of salvation. Let us all confess our sins to our people, and especially to Almighty God. Let us plead that atoning blood which cleanseth from all sin. Here is our only hope of pardon. It is yet a faithful saying, and worthy of all acceptation, that Christ Jesus came into the world to save sinners; and let us do works meet for repentance. In spite of sneers and obloquy and reproach, let us declare the whole counsel of God. Let us cast away all desire of reputation for scholarship, all love of distinction, and be content to preach the simple truths of the New Testament in all their breadth and length, whether men will hear or whether they will forbear. While doing all this, let us in humble faith rely upon the aid of the Spirit of God, which is promised everywhere to accompany the truth as it is in Jesus. We are nothing, and can do nothing; but when we faithfully utter the truth of God, he can do everything. Oh, what a reformation would follow such a baptism of the Spirit among the ministers of Christ! Our country would fall down before God in humble penitence, confessing its sins and pleading for pardon through the atonement of Christ. The chastening of God would have accomplished its purpose, and he would restore to us the blessings of peace on the principles of righteousness, which we by our sins have forfeited. Out of the infinite misery of this fearful contest, he would, in his own way, cause such an improvement in national character as should be more than a compensation for all that we have suffered. We should still be a day-star to the nations in darkness, the hope of those struggling for civil and religious freedom. God would be merciful to us, and bless us, that his way might be known upon earth, his saving health among all nations. The Lord hasten it in his time, and to his name shall be the glory.

Yours, very truly.

The End.

WORKS BY DR. TWEEDIE.

GLAD TIDINGS; or, The Gospel of Peace. A series of Daily Meditations for Christian Disciples. By Rev. W. K. TWEEDIE, D. D. With an elegant Illustrated Title-page. 16mo, cloth. 63 cents.

These meditations, though brief, are comprehensive and weighty. It is remarkable for condensation, for a deep evangelical tone, and for putting itself into direct contact with the conscience and the heart. — *Albany Argus.*

We heartily wish this little book were in every Christian family, and could be carefully read through by every Christian. — *N. Y. Evangelist.*

This sweet little volume challenges our warmest commendation. Every page glows with Christian example and goodness. The perusal of one chapter will awake a keener relish for the commencement of another. The *Frontispiece*, representing the shepherds' watch of their flocks by night, is sublimely beautiful. — *Lawrence Courier.*

A LAMP TO THE PATH; or, the Bible in the Heart, the Home, and the Market-place. With an elegant Illustrated Title-page. 16mo, cloth. 63 cents.

The power, the beauty, and the necessity of religion in the heart, the home, the workshop, the market-place, the professions, and in social intercourse, are happily illustrated. It is a jewel, and should enrich every family library. The last chapter is worthy of being engraven, as with the point of a diamond, on every human heart. — *Southern Literary Messenger.*

This little volume brings Christianity home to the bosoms and business of men. It is a lucid, impressive, and beautiful exposition of Christian obligations. — *Albany Argus.*

SEED-TIME AND HARVEST; or, Sow Well and Reap Well. A Book for the Young. With an elegant Illustrated Title-page. 16mo, cloth. 63 cents.

An excellent book, more particularly designed for young readers; but persons of all ages may derive pleasure and profit from its perusal. — *N. Y. Commercial.*

No person can read it attentively, without feeling that there is an importance attached even to what seem to be his most indifferent actions. — *Puritan Rec.*

A most precious volume this to the young, taking their first step and first look in life; teaching them that if they would reap well, they must sow well; that if they would enjoy an old age of honor, they must be trained in youth to virtue. — *Dr. Sprague, Albany Spectator.*

THE MORN OF LIFE; or, Examples of Female Excellence. A Book for Young Ladies. 16mo, cloth. *In press.*

☞ The above works, by Dr. Tweedie, are of uniform size and style. They are most charming, pious, and instructive works, beautifully gotten up, and well adapted for "gift-books."

FAMILY WORSHIP; or, the Morning and Evening Sacrifice. One volume. Octavo, cloth. *In press.*

VALUABLE WORKS.

THE SUFFERING SAVIOUR; or, Meditations on the Last Days of Christ. By Fred. W. Krummacher, D.D., Chaplain to the King of Prussia, and author of "Elijah the Tishbite," etc. Translated under the express sanction of the author, by Samuel Jackson. 12mo, cloth. $1.25.

The style of the author need not be described to those who have read his 'Elijah; and whoever has not read an evangelical book of our own time that has passed through many editions in German, English, French, Dutch, Danish, had better order the Chinese edition, which has recently appeared. * * * We like the book—love it, rather—for the vivid perception and fervid emotion with which it brings us to the Suffering Saviour."—New York Independent.

"Krummacher is himself again! Till the present work appeared, he had done nothing equal to his first one, 'Elijah, the Tishbite.' In the present he comes upon the literary firmament in his old fire and glory, 'like a re-appearing star.' The translator has done his work admirably. * * * Much of the narrative is given with thrilling vividness, and pathos, and beauty. Marking as we proceeded, several passages for quotation, we found them in the end so numerous, that we must refer the reader to the work itself."—News of the Churches (Scottish).

THE PROGRESS OF BAPTIST PRINCIPLES IN THE LAST HUNDRED YEARS. By T. F. Curtis, Professor of Theology in Lewisburg University, Pa. 12mo, cloth. $1.25.

This work is divided into three books. The first exhibits the progress of Baptist Principles, now conceeded in theory by the most enlighted of other denominations.

The second presents a view of the progress of principles still controverted.

The third sets forth the progress of principles always held by evangelical Christians, but more consistently by Baptists.

It is a work that invites the candid consideration of all denomitions. The aim has been to draw a wide distinction between parties and opinions. Hence the object of this volume is not to exhibit or defend the Baptists, but their principles."

"The principles referred to are such as these: Freedom of conscience and Separation of Church and State; a Converted Church Membership; Sacraments inoperative without Choice and Faith; Believers the only Scriptural Subjects of Baptism; Immersion always the Baptism of the New Testament; Infant Baptism Injurious; Open Communion Unwise and Injurious. To show the progress of these principles, statistics are given, from which we learn that in 1792 there was but one Baptist Communicant in the United States to every fifty-six inhabitants, while in 1854 there was one to every thirty inhabitants. The Baptists have more than one quarter of the whole Church accommodation in the United States. * * * The entire work is written with ability and unfailing good temper."—Quarterly Journal American Unitarian Association.

"The good temper of the author of this volume is obvious; the method of arranging his materials for effect admirable."—Presbyterian.

"We know of no man in our Churches better fitted to prepare a fair exhibition of 'Baptist Principles.' He is no controversialist; and his discussions are in most refreshing contrast with many, both of Baptist defenders and their opponents."—Southern Baptist.

"The work exhibits ample learning, vigorous argumentative power, and an excellent spirit toward those whose views it controverts. Apart from its theological bearings, it possesses not a little historical interest."—N. Y. Tribune.

"The aim of the work is important, the plan ingenious, yet simple and natural, the author's preparation for it apparently thorough and conscientious, and his spirit excellent."—Watchman and Reflector. (r)

MODERN ATHEISM.

Under its Forms of Pantheism, Materialism, Secularism, Development, and Natural Laws. By JAMES BUCHANAN, D.D., LL.D. 12mo, cloth, $1.25.

The Author of this work is the successor of Dr. Chalmers in the Chair of Divinity in the New College, Edinburgh, and the intellectual leader of the Scottish Free Church.

HUGH MILLER, AUTHOR OF "OLD RED SANDSTONE," &c., &c. — The work is one of the most readable and solid which we have ever perused.

THE "NEWS OF THE CHURCHES." — It is a work of which nothing less can be said, than that, both in spirit and substance, style and argument, it fixes irreversibly the name of the author as a leading classic in the Christian literature of Britain.

HOWARD MALCOM, D. D., PRESIDENT OF LEWISBURG UNIVERSITY. — I have found no work so helpful to me as this as a teacher of metaphysics and morals. I know of nothing which will answer for a substitute. The public specially need such a book at this time when atheism is being spread abroad with all earnestness, supported, at least in some places, both by church influence and university honors. I cannot but hope that a work so timely, scholarly, and complete, will do much good.

One of the most scholarly and profound productions of modern Christian literature. — WORCESTER TRANSCRIPT.

Dr. Buchanan has earned a high and well-deserved reputation as a classical writer and close logical reasoner. He deals heavy, deadly blows on atheism in all its various forms. — CHRISTIAN SECRETARY.

His analyses of the doctrines held by the various schools of modern atheism are admirable, and his criticism original and profound. It is an attractive as well as a solid book; and he who peruses a few of its pages is, as it were, irresistibly drawn on to a thorough reading of the book. — BOSTON PORTFOLIO.

The style is very felicitous, and the reasoning clear and cogent. The opposing theories are fairly stated and combated with remarkable ease and skill. Even when the argument falls within the range of science, it is so happily stated that no intelligent reader can fail to understand it. — BOSTON JOURNAL.

It is justly described as "a great argument," "magnificent in its strength, order, and beauty," in a defence of truth and against the variant theories of atheism. It reviews the doctrines of the different schools of modern Atheism, gives a fair statement of their theories, answers and refutes them, never evading, but meeting and crushing their arguments. — PHILA. CHRISTIAN OBSERVER.

Dr. Buchanan is candid and impartial, evades no argument, undertakes no opposing view, but meets his antagonists with the quiet and unswerving confidence of a locomotive on iron tracks, pretty sure to crush them. — CHRISTIAN REGISTER.

We hail this production of a master mind as a lucid, vigorous, discriminating, and satisfactory refutation of the various false philosophies which have appeared in modern times to allure ingenuous youth to their destruction. His refutation is a clear stream of light from beginning to end. — PHILA. PRESBYTERIAN.

We recommend "Modern Atheism" as a book for the times, and as having special claims on theological students. — UNIVERSALIST QUARTERLY.

It is remarkable for the clearness with which it apprehends and the fairness with which it states, not less than for the ability with which it replies to, the schemes of unbelief in its various modern forms. It clears away, one by one, the mists which the Devil has conjured around the great doctrines of our Faith, by the help of some of his ingenious modern coadjutors, and leaves the truth of God standing in its serene and pristine majesty— CONGREGATIONALIST.

The work is a masterly defence of faith against dogmatic unbelief on the one hand, and that universal skepticism on the other. — N. Y. CHRISTIAN CHRONICLE.

NEW WORKS.

THE BETTER LAND; or, The Believer's Journey and Future Home. By Rev. A. C. Thompson. 12mo, cloth. 85 cents.

Contents. — The Pilgrimage; Clusters of Eschol; Waymarks; Glimpses of the Land; The Passage; The Recognition of Friends; The Heavenly Banquet; Children in Heaven; Society of Angels; Society of the Saviour; Heavenly Honor and Riches; No Tears in Heaven; Holiness of Heaven; Activity in Heaven; Resurrection Body; Perpetuity of Bliss in Heaven.

A most charming and instructive book for all now journeying to the "Better Land."

THE SCHOOL OF CHRIST; or, Christianity viewed in its Leading Aspects. By the Rev. A. L. R. Foote, author of "Incidents in the Life of our Saviour," etc. 16mo, cloth. 50 cts.

"It is one of the few books that we feel free to recommend." — Meth. Protestant.

"The author presents Christianity, in its various aspects, with skill and power." — Presbyterian.

"Christians of all names will read it with deep interest." — Christ. Chronicle.

"It shows throughout a discriminating and thoroughly disciplined mind." — Puritan Recorder.

MY MOTHER; or, Recollections of Maternal Influence. By a New England Clergyman. 12mo, cloth. 75 cents.

This is a new and enlarged edition of a work that was first published in 1849. It passed rapidly through three editions, when the sale was arrested by the embarrassment of the publisher. The author has now revised it, and added another chapter, so that it comes before the public with the essential claims of a new work. . . . . It is the picture of a quiet New England Family, so drawn and colored as to subserve the ends of domestic education. . . . . . The author has already distinguished himself in various walks of literature; but from motives of delicacy towards the still surviving characters of the book, he chooses for the present to conceal his name. . . . . A writer of wide celebrity says of the book, in a note to the publisher — "It is one of those rare pictures, painted from life, with the exquisite skill of one of the old masters, which so seldom present themselves to the amateur."

MEMORIES OF A GRANDMOTHER. By a Lady of Massachusetts. 16mo, cloth. 50 cents.

"My path lies in a valley which I have sought to adorn with flowers. Shadows from the hills cover it, but I make my own sunshine."

"The little volume is gracefully and beautifully written." — Journal.

"Not unworthy the genius of a Dickens." — Transcript.

THE TEACHER'S LAST LESSON. A Memoir of Martha Whiting, late of the Charlestown Female Seminary, consisting chiefly of Extracts from her Journal, interspersed with Reminiscences and Suggestive Reflections. By Catharine N. Badger, an Associate Teacher. With a Portrait, and an Engraving of the Seminary. 12mo, cloth. $1.00 Second edition.

The subject of this Memoir was, for a quarter of a century, at the head of one of the most celebrated Female Seminaries in the country. During that period she educated more than three thousand young ladies. She was a kindred spirit to Mary Lyon, the celebrated founder of Mount Holyoke Seminary, with whom, for strength of character, eminent piety, devotion to her calling, and extraordinary success therein, she well deserves to be ranked.

(o)

Gould and Lincoln's Publications.

(SCIENTIFIC.)

ANNUAL OF SCIENTIFIC DISCOVERY. 11 vols., from 1850–1860. By D. A. WELLS, A. M. With Portraits of distinguished men. 12mo. $1.25 each.

THE PLURALITY OF WORLDS; a new edition, with the author's reviews of his reviewers. 12mo. $1.00.

COMPARATIVE ANATOMY OF THE ANIMAL KINGDOM. By Profs. SIEBOLD and STANNIUS. Tr. by W. I. BURNETT, M. D. 8vo. $3.00.

HUGH MILLER'S WORKS. *TESTIMONY OF THE ROCKS.* With Illustrations. 12mo, cloth. $1.25.

——— *FOOTPRINTS OF THE CREATOR.* With Illustrations. Memoir by LOUIS AGASSIZ. 12mo, cloth. $1.00.

——— *THE OLD RED SANDSTONE.* With Illustrations, etc. 12mo, cloth. $1.25.

——— *MY SCHOOLS AND SCHOOLMASTERS.* An Autobiography. Full-length Portrait of Author. 12mo, cloth. $1.25.

——— *FIRST IMPRESSIONS OF ENGLAND AND ITS PEOPLE.* With fine Portrait. 12mo, cloth. $1.00.

——— *CRUISE OF THE BETSEY.* A Ramble among the Fossiliferous Deposits of the Hebrides. 12mo, cl. $1.25.

——— *POPULAR GEOLOGY.* 12mo, cl. $1.25.

HUGH MILLER'S WORKS, 7 vols., embossed cloth, with box, $8.25.

UNITED STATES EXPLORING EXPEDITION. WILKES. Vol. XII., Mollusca and Shells. By A. A. GOULD, M. D. 4to. $10 00.

THE NATURAL HISTORY OF THE HUMAN SPECIES. By C. HAMILTON SMITH. With Elegant Illustrations. Introduction, containing an abstract of the views of eminent writers on the subject, by S. KNEELAND, M. D. 12mo. $1.25.

THE CAMEL. His organization, habits, and uses, with reference to his introduction into the United States. By G. P. MARSH. 12mo. 63c.

INFLUENCE OF THE HISTORY OF SCIENCE UPON INTELLECTUAL EDUCATION. By W. WHEWELL, D. D. 12mo. 25 cents.

SPIRITUALISM TESTED; or, the Facts of its History Classified, and their cause in Nature verified from Ancient and Modern Testimonies. By GEO. W. SAMSON, D. D. 16mo, cloth. 38 cents.

Gould and Lincoln's Publications.

(LITERARY.)

THE PURITANS; or, the Court, Church, and Parliament of England. By SAMUEL HOPKINS. 3 vols., 8vo, cloth. $2.50 per vol.

HISTORICAL EVIDENCES OF THE TRUTH OF THE SCRIPTURE RECORDS, STATED ANEW, with Special Reference to the Doubts and Discoveries of Modern Times. Bampton Lecture for 1859. By GEORGE RAWLINSON. 12mo, cloth. $1.00.

CHRIST IN HISTORY. By ROBERT TURNBULL, D. D. A New and Enlarged Edition. 12mo, cloth. $1 25.

THE CHRISTIAN LIFE; Social and Individual. By PETER BAYNE. 12mo, cloth. $1.25.

ESSAYS IN BIOGRAPHY AND CRITICISM. By PETER BAYNE. Arranged in two series, or parts. 2 vols., 12mo, cloth. $1.25 each.

THE GREYSON LETTERS. By HENRY ROGERS, Author of the "Eclipse of Faith." 12mo, cloth. $1.25.

CHAMBERS' WORKS. *CYCLOPÆDIA OF ENGLISH LITERATURE.* Selections from English Authors, from the earliest to the present time. 2 vols., 8vo, cloth. $5.00.

——— *MISCELLANY OF USEFUL AND ENTERTAINING KNOWLEDGE.* 10 vols., 16mo, cloth. $7.50.

——— *HOME BOOK;* or, Pocket Miscellany. 6 vols. 16mo, cloth. $3.00.

MISCELLANIES. By WILLIAM R. WILLIAMS, D. D. 12mo, cl. $1.25.

ANCIENT LITERATURE AND ART. Essays and Letters from Eminent Philologists. By Profs. SEARS, EDWARDS, and FELTON. 12mo, cloth. $1.25.

MODERN FRENCH LITERATURE. By L. RAYMOND DE VERICOUR. Revised, with Notes by W. S. CHASE. 12mo, cloth. $1.25.

BRITISH NOVELISTS AND THEIR STYLES. By DAVID MASSON, M. A., Author of Life of Milton. 16mo, cloth. 75 cents.

THE HALLIG; or, the Sheepfold in the Waters. Translated from the German of BIERNATSKI, by Mrs. GEORGE P. MARSH. 12mo, cloth. $1.00.

MANSEL'S MISCELLANIES; including "Prolegomina Logica," "Metaphysics," "Limits of Demonstrative Evidence," "Philosophy of Kant," etc. 12mo. *In press.*

Gould and Lincoln's Publications.

(BIOGRAPHICAL.)

LIFE OF JOHN MILTON, in connection with the Political, Ecclesiastical, and Literary History of his time. By DAVID MASSON, M. A. 3 vols., 8vo. Vol. I., cloth. $2.75.

LIFE AND CORRESPONDENCE OF REV. DANIEL WILSON, D. D., late Bishop of Calcutta. By Rev. JOSIAH BATEMAN. With portraits, map, and illustrations. 1 vol., royal octavo. $3.00.

LIFE AND CORRESPONDENCE OF THE LATE AMOS LAWRENCE. By W. R. LAWRENCE, M. D. 8vo, cloth. $1.50. 12mo, cloth. $1.00.

DR. GRANT AND THE MOUNTAIN NESTORIANS. By Rev. THOMAS LAURIE, his surviving associate. 12mo, cloth. $1.25.

MEMOIR OF THE LIFE AND TIMES OF ISAAC BACKUS. By ALVAH HOVEY, D. D. 12mo, cloth. $1.25.

LIFE OF JAMES MONTGOMERY. By Mrs. H. C. KNIGHT, Author of "Lady Huntington and her Friends." 12mo, cloth. $1.25.

MY MOTHER; or, Recollections of Maternal Influence. By a New England Clergyman. 12mo, cloth. 75 cents.

LIFE AND CORRESPONDENCE OF JOHN FOSTER. By JOHN E. RYLAND. 2 vols. in one, 12mo, cloth. $1.25.

PHILIP DODDRIDGE. His Life and Labors. By JOHN STOUGHTON, D. D. 16mo, cloth. 60 cents.

MEMOIR OF ANN H. JUDSON. By Rev. J. D. KNOWLES. 18mo, cloth. 58 cents.

MEMOIR OF GEORGE D. BOARDMAN. By Rev. A. KING. Introduction by W. R. WILLIAMS, D. D. 12mo, cloth. 75 cents.

LIFE OF GODFREY WILLIAM VON LEIBNITZ. By JOHN M. MACKIE. 16mo, cloth. 75 cents.

TEACHER'S LAST LESSON; Memoir of MARTHA WHITING, of Charlestown Female Sem. By C. N. BADGER. 12mo, cloth. $1.00.

MEMOIR OF HENRIETTA SHUCK, the first Female Missionary to China. By Rev. J. B. JETER, D. D. 18mo, cloth. 50 cents.

MEMOIR OF REV. WILLIAM G. CROCKER, Missionary to West Africa. By R. B. MEDBURY. 18mo, cloth. 63 cents.

www.ingramcontent.com/pod-product-compliance
Lightning Source LLC
LaVergne TN
LVHW011202110826
845150LV00006B/1296

9781425518745